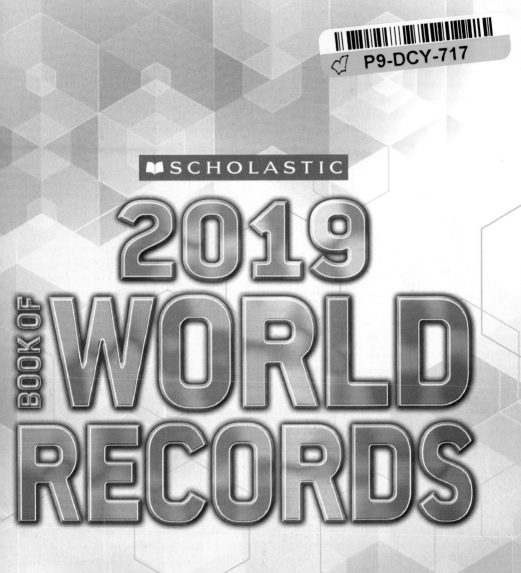

P9-DCY-717

SCHOLASTIC

2019

BOOK OF WORLD RECORDS

BY
CYNTHIA O'BRIEN
ABIGAIL MITCHELL
MICHAEL BRIGHT
DONALD SOMMERVILLE

If you purchased this book without a cover, you should be aware that this book is stolen property. It was reported as "unsold and destroyed" to the publisher, and neither the author nor the publisher has received any payment for this "stripped book."

Copyright © 2018 by Scholastic Inc.

All rights reserved. Published by Scholastic Inc., *Publishers since 1920.*
SCHOLASTIC and associated logos are trademarks and/or registered trademarks of Scholastic Inc.

Due to this book's publication date, the majority of statistics are current as of May 2018. The publisher does not have any control over and does not assume any responsibility for author or third-party websites or their content.

No part of this publication may be reproduced, stored in a retrieval system, or transmitted in any form or by any means, electronic, mechanical, photocopying, recording, or otherwise, without written permission of the publisher. For information regarding permission, write to Scholastic Inc., Attention: Permissions Department, 557 Broadway, New York, NY 10012.

This book was created and produced by Toucan Books Limited.
Text: Michael Bright, Abigail Mitchell, Cynthia O'Brien, Donald Sommerville
Designer: Lee Riches
Editor: Anna Southgate
Proofreader: Nancy Dickmann
Index: Marie Lorimer
Toucan would like to thank Stephen Chin for picture research.

ISBN 978-1-338-30785-6

10 9 8 7 6 5 4 3 2 1   18 19 20 21 22

Printed in the U.S.A. 40

First printing, 2018

CONTENTS

1

MUSIC MAKERS

MUSIC MAKERS
TRENDING#

BEYONCÉ'S BABIES
Queen B's Instagram announcements

Kneeling in front of a rose-studded wreath and wearing a green veil, Beyoncé announced that she was expecting twins in an Instagram post in February 2017. The post went viral, notching up 7.2 million likes in less than twenty hours. The twins, Rumi and Sir, arrived safely in June, and Beyoncé used Instagram for their first public photo the following month. The post received more than 10 million likes.

BRUNO TAKES ALL
Award glory at the Grammys

Bruno Mars was nominated for six awards at the 2018 Grammys and won all of them! Three were the top prizes of Album, Record, and Song of the Year. The awards were given for his album *24K Magic*, its title track, and "That's What I Like," a song he wrote in collaboration with seven others.

SPIN THOSE DISKS!
A vinyl revival

According to global data collector Nielsen, vinyl records made a comeback in 2017, accounting for 14 percent of all physical album sales in the United States. Forty million albums sold on vinyl across the globe. This may seem a low figure compared to the meganumbers that sell digitally, but it marks the biggest sales of vinyl since the 1980s. In the United States, the most popular vinyl album of 2017 was a re-release of The Beatles' *Sgt. Pepper's Lonely Hearts Club Band.*

YOUTUBE'S TOP-TRENDING VIDEO CLIP
The Mask Singer

With more than 182 million views, an excerpt from a Thai TV show, *The Mask Singer*, was YouTube's top-trending video of 2017. A "view" counts as any time the clip is watched, shared, liked, or commented on. *The Mask Singer* is a singing competition where celebrities perform in disguise. In this clip, a singer in an oyster costume sang a song that combined a ballad style with rapping. It drove the audience wild.

FROM WALMART TO COACHELLA
Yodeling boy

In April 2018, Mason Ramsey from Golconda, Illinois, wowed the Internet when he sang Hank Williams Sr.'s "Lovesick Blues" in a Walmart store, throwing in a few yodels to boot. His stunt went viral, earning him an invitation to appear on *The Ellen DeGeneres Show*, and the chance to perform at the Coachella music festival. Justin Bieber was in the crowd and took a few minutes to talk to Mason in person.

MOST DOWNLOADED **song**

"SHAPE OF YOU"

With a massive 1.4 billion streams in total, "Shape of You" by British singer-songwriter Ed Sheeran was Spotify's most-streamed song of 2017. According to the music-streaming service, Sheeran was also the most-streamed artist of the year, with forty-seven million listeners a month. Recognizable by his shock of ruffled red hair, Sheeran's success comes in a year of impressive collaborations with other artists, including Beyoncé, Taylor Swift, and Eminem. Drake, who held the top spot for most-streamed artist in 2015 and 2016, failed to make it into the top five most-streamed songs, while "Despacito" is featured twice, having been released in two versions.

MOST STREAMED SONGS 2017

Ed Sheeran, "Shape of You"

Luis Fonsi & Daddy Yankee (ft. Justin Bieber), "Despacito"

Luis Fonsi (ft. Daddy Yankee), "Despacito"

The Chainsmokers (ft. Coldplay), "Something Just Like This"

DJ Khaled (ft. Justin Bieber, Quavo, Lil Wayne, and Chance the Rapper), "I'm The One"

TOP-SELLING album

America's top-selling album of 2017 was Ed Sheeran's ÷ (*Divide*). According to the data-tracking company Nielsen, the title earned 2.76 **million** equivalent album units during the year, with 1.1 million of those resulting from traditional album sales. With Sheeran's first two albums, + (*Plus*) and × (*Multiply*), ÷ (*Divide*) completes a mathematical trio. While Sheeran reigned supreme in terms of figures that combined traditional album **sales with** streaming equivalents, his sales were bested by Taylor Swift's *Reputation* when it came to traditional album sales alone. Swift amassed 1.9 million compared to Sheeran's 1.1 milllion.

Averaging more than 30,000 views per minute, three million per hour, and 43.2 million in total, Taylor Swift's video for her hit song "Look What You Made Me Do" was 2017's most-viewed online music video in twenty-four hours. Released on YouTube on August 29, the video shows a darker side to Swift than fans are used to and opens with the star emerging zombie-like from a grave. The first song released from Swift's *Reputation* album, it was intended as a response to media criticism and the behavior of other stars. Its record number of views overtook previous record-holder Psy's "Gentleman," which had thirty-six million views in its first twenty-four hours in 2013.

MOST-VIEWED
online music video

Taylor Swift
"LOOK WHAT YOU MADE ME DO"

TOP-EARNING tour U2

The tour that earned the most money in 2017 was U2's "Joshua Tree Tour," which celebrated the thirtieth anniversary of the band's much-loved 1987 album of the same name. Claiming sales of 2.71 million tickets worldwide, the tour grossed an incredible $316 million from its fifty shows held in thirty-eight cities. Releasing its first single in 1979, the Irish rock band has been performing for almost forty years and holds the record for the highest-grossing tour of all time. Their "360° Tour" of 2009–11 grossed $736 million in total— more than double that of the "Joshua Tree Tour."

TOP-EARNING TOURS 2017
Revenue in millions of U.S. dollars

U2 316

Guns N' Roses 292.5

Coldplay 238

Bruno Mars 200.1

Metallica 152.8

FIRST RAPPER TO TOP

Billboard 100 chart

DRAKE

Drake released his album *If You're Reading This It's Too Late* through iTunes on February 12, 2015. The digital album sold 495,000 units in its first week and entered the *Billboard* 100 at no. 1, making Drake the first rap artist ever to top the chart. The album also helped Drake secure another record: the most hits on the *Billboard* 100 at one time.

On March 7, 2015, Drake had fourteen hit songs on the chart, matching the record the Beatles have held since 1964. Since releasing his first hit single, "Best I Ever Had," in 2009, Drake has seen many of his singles go multiplatinum, including "Hotline Bling," which sold 41,000 copies in its first week and had 18 weeks at no. 1 on the *Billboard* 100

TOP GROUP/ DUO

THE CHAINSMOKERS

TOP GROUP/DUOS 2017
1 The Chainsmokers
2 BTS
3 Coldplay
4 Migos
5 Imagine Dragons

Singing duo Andrew Taggart and Alex Pall, better known as The Chainsmokers, were the number one group/duo of 2017, according to *Billboard*. The pair's single "Something Just Like This," a collaboration with British band Coldplay, placed at no. 5 in the *Billboard* Top 100 songs of 2017, while "Closer," featuring Hallsey, placed at no. 7. The New York City–based electronic duo were the only artists to have two tracks in the top ten, and just one of two groups, along with Imagine Dragons. "Closer" had been a hit in 2016, one of two tracks released from the band's debut album, *Memories . . . do not open*. The second was "Don't Let Me Down."

TOP-SELLING recording THE group BEATLES

TOP-SELLING RECORDING GROUPS IN THE UNITED STATES
Albums sold in millions

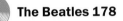 **The Beatles 178**

Led Zeppelin 111.5

Eagles 101

Pink Floyd 75

AC/DC 72

The Beatles continue to hold the record for the bestselling recording group in the United States with 178 million albums sold. The British band recorded their first album in September 1962 and made their *Billboard* debut with "I Want to Hold Your Hand." Before breaking up in 1969, the group had twenty number-one songs and recorded some of the world's most famous albums, including *Sgt. Pepper's Lonely Hearts Club Band*.

SHORTEST CONCERT ever
WHITE STRIPES

In St. John's, Newfoundland, the White Stripes's lead, Jack White, played just one note—a C sharp. The White Stripes had played at least one show in each of Canada's thirteen provinces and territories, as well as "secret" shows in various venues. Die-hard fans found out about these secret shows through posts on the White Stripes message board, The Little Room.

The one-note show in Newfoundland was a secret event, though hundreds turned up to watch. The official end of the tour was a full set played later that night. *Under Great White Northern Lights*, released in 2010, is a documentary of the tour. The film features backstage moments as well as scenes from the live concerts, and an impromptu performance on a public bus.

15

BESTSELLING
digital song
of all time

On July 19, 2017, according to record producer Universal Music Latin Entertainment, the Latin song "Despacito" became the most-streamed track of all time, when it reached a colossal 4.6 billion global streams—a record achieved in just six months. The song, by Puerto Rican duo Luis Fonsi & Daddy Yankee, was a new version of a track they had released earlier in the year, but this time it featured Justin Bieber. The new version skyrocketed past Bieber's own record of 4.38 billion plays for his 2015 hit "Sorry." Besides its incredible streaming success, the original "Despacito" track won a Latin Grammy for best song of the year.

"DESPACITO"
LUIS FONSI & DADDY YANKEE

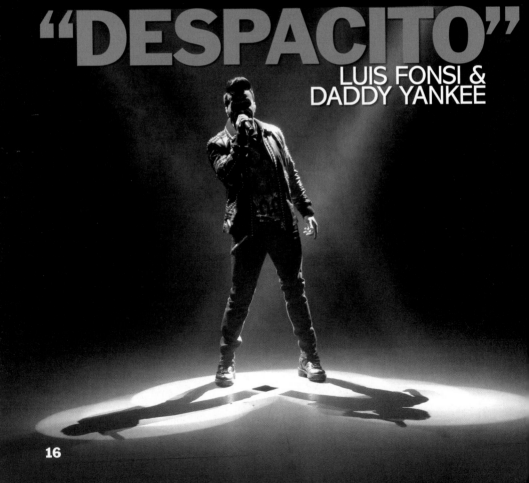

LONGEST-EVER
music video

"HAPPY"
BY PHARRELL

Pharrell Williams made history in November 2013 with the release of the first 24-hour music video—the longest music video ever. The video for Williams's hit song "Happy" is a four-minute track that plays on a loop 360 times. In addition to Williams, celebrities such as Jamie Foxx, Steve Carell, and Miranda Cosgrove make appearances in the video. In 2014, "Happy" broke records again, becoming the first single to top six *Billboard* charts in one year and becoming the year's bestselling song with 6,455,000 digital copies sold.

**TOP-EARNING
FEMALE SINGERS 2017**
In millions of U.S. dollars

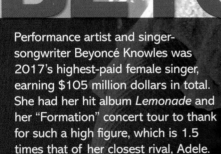

Beyoncé 105

Adele 69

Taylor Swift 44

Celine Dion 42

Jennifer Lopez 38

TOP-EARNING
female singer
BEYONCÉ

Performance artist and singer-songwriter Beyoncé Knowles was 2017's highest-paid female singer, earning $105 million dollars in total. She had her hit album *Lemonade* and her "Formation" concert tour to thank for such a high figure, which is 1.5 times that of her closest rival, Adele.

According to *Forbes*, Beyoncé was the world's second-highest-paid celebrity in 2017, while she and her rapper husband, Jay-Z, were the highest-paid celebrity couple—and this in a year when they took time off to celebrate the birth of their twins, Rumi and Sir.

TOP
radio song

"SHAPE OF YOU"
ED SHEERAN

Given that British singer-songwriter Ed Sheeran's "Shape of You" was Spotify's most-streamed hit of 2017, it comes as no surprise that the tune was also the most-played song on U.S. radio, with 1.115 million single radio plays across the twelve-month period. According to Nielsen's year-end report, Sheeran's popular track was the only song in the whole of 2017 to pass one million radio spins. Bruno Mars's "That's What I Like" was not far behind with

TOP RADIO SONGS IN 2017
Number of spins

Ed Sheeran, "Shape of You" 1,115,000

Bruno Mars, "That's What I Like" 959,000

The Chainsmokers and Coldplay, "Something Just Like This" 723,000

Zedd (ft. Alessia Cara), "Stay" 655,000

Alessia Cara, "Scars to Your Beautiful" 638,000

ACT WITH THE MOST
Country Music Awards
GEORGE STRAIT

"King of Country" George Strait won his first Country Music Award (CMA) in 1985 for Male Vocalist of the Year and Album of the Year. Since then, Strait has won an amazing twenty-three CMAs, including Entertainer of the Year in 2013. The country music superstar has thirty-three platinum or multiplatinum albums, and he holds the record for the most platinum certifications in country music. George Strait was inducted into the Country Music Hall of Fame in 2006.

MUSICIAN WITH THE MOST MTV Video Music Awards
BEYONCÉ

The queen of pop, Beyoncé, is the winningest VMA artist ever. She won eight MTV Video Music Awards in 2016 alone, pushing her ahead of Madonna's twenty VMA trophies and setting a new record of twenty-four VMA wins. The music video for "Formation," from Beyoncé's visual album *Lemonade*, won five awards, including the coveted prize for Video of the Year. With eight moon men from eleven nominations, Beyoncé tied the record for the most VMA wins in one year by a female solo artist, also held by Lady Gaga.

MUSICIAN WITH THE MOST MTV VIDEO MUSIC AWARDS

Beyoncé 24

Madonna 20

Lady Gaga 13

Peter Gabriel 13

Eminem 12

TOP
country song
"BODY LIKE A BACK ROAD"

TOP COUNTRY SONGS
Number of weeks at no. 1 on Hot Country Songs

♫ ♫ ♫ ♫ ♫ **Sam Hunt, "Body Like a Back Road" 34**

♫ ♫ ♫ ♫ **Florida Georgia Line, "Cruise" 25**

♫ ♫ ♫ **Leroy Van Dyke, "Walk On By" 19**

♫ ♫ **Florida Georgia Line, "H.O.L.Y." 18**

♫ **Thomas Rhett, "Die a Happy Man" 17**

Sam Hunt's "Body Like a Back Road" broke an all-time record for sitting at the top of *Billboard*'s Hot Country Songs and *Billboard*'s Country Streaming songs for thirty-four weeks apiece. The song outstripped former record-holder Florida Georgia Line's "Cruise" by an impressive nine weeks in Hot Country Songs. "Body Like a Back Road" was cowritten by Hunt and was released as a stand-alone track three years after the artist made his debut album, *Montevallo*, which has sold 1.3 million units to date.

BESTSELLING
country
album

FROM A ROOM, VOLUME 1

TOP-SELLING COUNTRY ALBUMS 2017
Number of units sold

Chris Stapleton, *From A Room, Volume 1* **658,000**

Chris Stapleton, *Traveller* **410,000**

Kenny Chesney, *Live in No Shoes Nation* **342,000**

Keith Urban, *Ripcord* **295,000**

Zac Brown Band, *Welcome Home* **292,000**

With a sound reminiscent of 1970s country classics, Chris Stapleton ended 2017 with not one, but two, top-selling country albums. After years of experience writing contemporary country hits for other artists—such as Thomas Rhett's upbeat "Crash and Burn"—Stapleton released his first studio album, *Traveller*, in 2015. After selling one million copies in 2016, *Traveller* continued to sell throughout 2017. Its sales were only bettered by Stapleton's second album, *From A Room, Volume 1*, which finished the year with 658,000 sales.

screen & STAGE

SCREEN & STAGE
TRENDING

ALL NEW AT MTV
Gender-neutral prizes

In 2017, for the first time ever, the MTV Movie & TV Awards chose not to consider gender when giving out the top prizes. Any artist—male, female, and gender nonbinary—found themselves in the running. The prize for Best Actor in a Movie went to Emma Watson for her performance in *Beauty and the Beast*, while Millie Bobby Brown claimed the award for Best Actor in a Show for her role as Eleven in *Stranger Things*.

MAKING TWITTER HISTORY
Black Panther

In March 2018, the celebrated movie *Black Panther* became the first film ever to be Tweeted about more than 35 million times. The most shared Tweet about the film was Kendrick Lamar's soundtrack announcement, which was Retweeted 240,000 times. Of the 35 million Tweets posted, the most Tweeted-about hashtags were #BlackPanther, #WakandaForever, and #Wakanda.

LA-LA BLOOPER
Mix-up at the Oscars

The prize for Best Picture at the 2017 Academy Awards went to *La La Land* . . . or did it? This was the announcement given by Warren Beatty and Faye Dunaway when, in fact, *Moonlight* had won the award. Jordan Horowitz, a *La La Land* producer, had to step in to correct the mistake, spawning a rash of memes on the Internet. It wasn't all bad for *La La Land*, which, having been nominated for fourteen Oscars in total, managed to take home six of them, including Best Director and Best Actress.

HAIR-RAISING ANTICS
Drew Barrymore in the world's widest wig

Appearing on *The Tonight Show* in January 2017, actor Drew Barrymore broke a Guinness World Record by wearing the world's widest wig. Measuring 7 feet, 4 inches wide, the wig had pretty red bows on either side of the center part. Barrymore was dwarfed by the hairpiece, which had to be placed on her head by no fewer than four people.

#WHAT'SMYSNACK
Chris Pratt's eating habits

Fancy an olive oil pistachio cake? No? Neither did Chris Pratt, it seems, according to his Instagram series #What'sMySnack. Faced with a strict dietary regime when filming *Jurassic World: Fallen Kingdom* in 2017, the actor made light of his snacks on Instagram. While eating sashimi—raw fish wrapped in seaweed—the star said: "This is one of those things where when you're as hungry as I am, everything tastes really good."

LONGEST-RUNNING
scripted TV show in the United States THE SIMPSONS

In 2017, *The Simpsons* entered a record twenty-ninth season, making it the longest-running American sitcom, cartoon, and scripted prime-time television show in history. The animated comedy, which first aired in December 1989, centers on the antics and everyday lives of the Simpson family. The show's creator, Matt Groening, named the characters after members in his own family, although he substituted Bart for his own name. In 2017, the show's guest stars included Kat Dennings and Rachel Bloom.

TV SHOW WITH THE MOST Emmy Awards

SATURDAY NIGHT LIVE

The variety show *Saturday Night Live* won nine Emmy Awards in 2017, including the award for Outstanding Variety Sketch Series. The late-night comedy show broadcasts live from New York City's Rockefeller Center on Saturday nights. A new celebrity host introduces the show each week and takes part in comedy skits with the regular cast. *Saturday Night Live* launched the careers of America's top comedians, including Will Ferrell, Tina Fey, and Kristen Wiig, many of whom return to the show regularly in guest spots. In this year's awards, Kate McKinnon won Outstanding Supporting Actress in a Comedy Series and Alec Baldwin won Outstanding Supporting Actor in a Comedy Series, for their frequent impressions of former First Lady Hillary Clinton and President Trump.

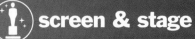
HIGHEST-PAID
TV actress SOFÍA VERGARA

For the second year running, *Modern Family*'s Sofía Vergara holds top spot for the highest-paid actress on television in 2017, earning $41.5 million. While one-quarter of Vergara's income comes from her role as Gloria Delgado-Pritchett in *Modern Family*, she also earns money from endorsements and licensing deals that include Avon, Pepsi, and CoverGirl. Vergara, who is originally from Colombia, has won four Screen Actors Guild Awards as part of the *Modern Family* cast for Outstanding Performance by an Ensemble in a Comedy Series.

TOP-EARNING TV ACTRESSES
In millions of U.S. dollars

Sofía Vergara 41.5

Kaley Cuoco 26

Mindy Kaling 13

Ellen Pompeo 13

Mariska Hargitay 12.5

CELEBRITY WITH THE MOST
Kids' Choice Awards
WILL SMITH

Will Smith has won 11 Kids' Choice Awards, including two Best Actor wins for his roles in *The Fresh Prince of Bel-Air* and *Hancock*. Will Smith's career took off with *The Fresh Prince of Bel-Air*, a sitcom that aired for six years in the 1990s. He went on to have a highly successful movie career, earning two Academy Award nominations for *The Pursuit of Happyness* and *Ali*. Nickelodeon introduced the Kids' Choice Awards in 1988—a highlight of the show is its tradition of "sliming" celebrity guests with green goo, often taking them by surprise.

CELEBRITIES WITH THE MOST KIDS' CHOICE AWARDS

Will Smith 11

Adam Sandler 10

Selena Gomez 10

Miley Cyrus 6

Amanda Bynes 6

MOST POPULAR TV show

NBC SUNDAY NIGHT FOOTBALL

According to Nielsen, *Sunday Night Football* had an average of 18.6 million viewers in 2017, making it America's top-rated show for a record seventh consecutive year. Since 1950, the only other show to come close to having such a long stretch at the top was *American Idol*, with six consecutive years. NBC *Sunday Night Football* has won numerous Sports Emmy Awards. Hosts include sports analyst Cris Collinsworth, the play-by-play commentator Al Michaels, and Michele Tafoya, the sideline reporter.

Jim Parsons was yet again TV's highest-paid actor in 2017, earning $27.5 million. Most of his income came from playing television's favorite physicist, Sheldon Cooper, in *The Big Bang Theory*. His costars Johnny Galecki, Simon Helberg, and Kunal Nayyar also made the top five—unsurprising, given that the sitcom was the second-most-watched show of the 2016–2017 season. Parsons appeared in numerous TV shows before getting his big break in 2006 with a lead role as Sheldon. He has since won four Emmy Awards for Outstanding Lead Actor in a Comedy Series.

HIGHEST-PAID
TV actor JIM
PARSONS

HIGHEST-PAID TV ACTORS
In millions of U.S. dollars

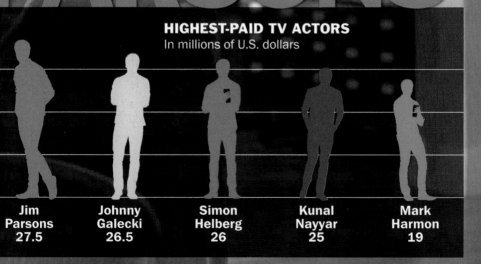

Jim Parsons	Johnny Galecki	Simon Helberg	Kunal Nayyar	Mark Harmon
27.5	26.5	26	25	19

MOVIE WITH THE HIGHEST production costs

MOVIES WITH THE HIGHEST PRODUCTION COSTS
In millions of U.S. dollars

Pirates of the Caribbean: On Stranger Tides 378.5

Pirates of the Caribbean: At World's End 300

Justice League 300

Avengers: Age of Ultron 279.9

John Carter 263.7

Pirates of the Caribbean: On Stranger Tides cost a huge $378.5 million to produce, almost $80 million more than *Pirates of the Caribbean: At World's End*, released four years earlier. The 2011 movie was the fourth in Walt Disney's Pirates of the Caribbean franchise starring Johnny Depp as Captain Jack Sparrow. In this installment of the wildly popular series, Captain Jack goes in search of the Fountain of Youth. Depp earned $55.5 million for the role, and the movie went on to earn $1.04 billion worldwide. In 2017, Johnny Depp returned to play Captain Jack in *Pirates of the Caribbean: Dead Men Tell No Tales*, the latest title in the franchise.

PIRATES OF THE CARIBBEAN ON STRANGER TIDES

MOST SUCCESSFUL
movie franchise

MARVEL CINEMATIC UNIVERSE

The Marvel Comics superhero movie franchise has grossed more than $15.7 billion worldwide—and counting! This impressive total includes ticket sales from the huge hits of 2018, *Black Panther* and *Avengers: Infinity War*. Just as it looked as if *Black Panther* was going to be the Marvel film of the year, grossing $1.34 billion worldwide within three months of its release, *Avengers: Infinity War* hit the movie screens. The movie took $1.82 billion worldwide in its first month, beating *The Avengers* 2012 record of $1.52 billion to claim title to the top-grossing movie in the Marvel franchise.

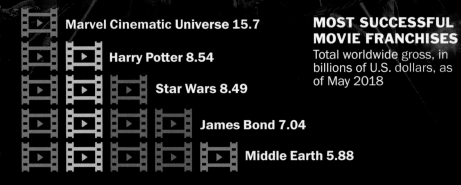

Marvel Cinematic Universe 15.7

Harry Potter 8.54

Star Wars 8.49

James Bond 7.04

Middle Earth 5.88

MOST SUCCESSFUL MOVIE FRANCHISES
Total worldwide gross, in billions of U.S. dollars, as of May 2018

movies with the most OSCARS

MOVIES WITH THE MOST OSCARS

Ben-Hur (1959) 11

Titanic (1997) 11

The Lord of the Rings: The Return of the King (2003) 11

West Side Story (1961) 10

Gigi (1958); The Last Emperor (1987); The English Patient (1996) 9

It's a three-way tie for the movie with the most Academy Awards: *Ben-Hur*, *Titanic*, and *The Lord of the Rings: The Return of the King* have each won eleven Oscars, including Best Picture and Best Director. The 1959 biblical epic *Ben-Hur* was the first to achieve this record number of wins. *Titanic*, based on the real 1912 disaster, won numerous Oscars for its striking visual and sound effects. *The Lord of the Rings: The Return of the King* was the third in a trilogy based on the books by J. R. R. Tolkien. It is the only movie of the top three to win in every category in which it was nominated.

SO WHO'S OSCAR?

Every year the Academy of Motion Picture Arts and Sciences presents awards in recognition of the greatest achievements in the film industry. Those actors, directors, screenwriters, and producers lucky enough to win each receive a highly prized golden statuette, aka "Oscar." No one really knows where the name comes from, although it is thought to have originated among the Hollywood greats of the 1930s—Bette Davis and Walt Disney have been credited, among others. Either way, "Oscar" became the official nickname for the Academy Award in 1939.

YOUNGEST ACTRESS nominated for an Oscar

QUVENZHANÉ WALLIS

At nine years old, Quvenzhané Wallis became the youngest-ever Academy Award nominee. The actress received the Best Actress nomination in 2013 for her role as Hushpuppy in *Beasts of the Southern Wild*. Although Wallis did not win the Oscar, she went on to gain forty-one more nominations and win twenty-four awards at various industry award shows. In 2015, she received a Golden Globe Best Actress nomination for her role in *Annie*. Wallis was five years old when she auditioned for Hushpuppy (the minimum age was six), and she won the part over four thousand other candidates.

Justin Henry was just seven years old when he received a Best Supporting Actor nomination for *Kramer vs. Kramer* in 1980. His neighbor, a casting director, suggested that Henry try out for the part. Although the young actor lost out on the Oscar, *Kramer vs. Kramer* won several Oscars, including Best Actor for Dustin Hoffman, Best Actress in a Supporting Role for Meryl Streep, and Best Picture. Justin Henry appeared in a few other films before leaving acting to finish his education. He then returned to acting in the 1990s.

YOUNGEST ACTOR
nominated for an Oscar
JUSTIN HENRY

MOVIES WITH THE MOST SUCCESSFUL DOMESTIC OPENING WEEKEND
Weekend earnings, in millions of U.S. dollars

Star Wars: The Force Awakens (12/18/15) 248

Star Wars: The Last Jedi (15/12/17) 220

Jurassic World (6/12/15) 208.8

Marvel's The Avengers (5/4/12) 207.4

Avengers: Age of Ultron (5/1/15) 191.2

Star Wars: Episode VII: The Force Awakens broke box-office records in December 2015 as the movie with the most successful opening weekend in the United States and the movie that earned the most money in a single day. The movie's opening weekend of December 18–20, 2015, earned an incredible $247,966,675 in the United States and $528,966,675 worldwide. The film broke another record when it took just twelve days to reach $1 billion worldwide, faster than any film in history. On its opening day alone, *Star Wars: The Force Awakens* earned over $119 million. New stars Daisy Ridley, John Boyega, and Oscar Isaac joined original cast members Carrie Fisher, Harrison Ford, and Mark Hamill. Carrie Fisher, the actress who played Princess Leia, passed away in 2016, but not before filming scenes for the next movie in the franchise, *The Last Jedi*. Released in December 2017, with Fisher's scenes remaining intact, the film instantly became the movie with the second-most successful opening weekend, earning $220 million at the box office.

STAR WARS: EPISODE VII: THE FORCE AWAKENS smashes BOX OFFICE RECORDS!

STAR WARS STATS:

11,000,000

PRODUCTION COSTS FOR *STAR WARS: EPISODE IV: A NEW HOPE*: $11 million

245,000,000

PRODUCTION COSTS FOR *STAR WARS: EPISODE VII: THE FORCE AWAKENS*: $245 million

1,074,500,000

APPROXIMATE PRODUCTION COSTS FOR NINE STAR WARS MOVIES TO DATE: $1 billion

ACTRESSES WITH THE MOST

MTV Movie Awards

JENNIFER LAWRENCE AND KRISTEN STEWART

ACTRESSES WITH THE MOST MTV MOVIE AWARDS

★ ★ ★ ★ ★ **Jennifer Lawrence 7**

★ ★ ★ ★ ★ **Kristen Stewart 7**

★ ★ ★ **Shailene Woodley 5**

★ ★ **Sandra Bullock 4**

★ ★ **Alicia Silverstone 4**

Jennifer Lawrence and Kristen Stewart share the title of actress with the most MTV Movie Awards. Stewart won all seven of her awards for her role as Bella Swan in the movie adaptations of the Twilight franchise—including four Best Kiss awards with costar Robert Pattinson. Lawrence's seventh award was for Best Hero, which she won in 2016 for her role as Katniss Everdeen in the fourth installment of the popular Hunger Games franchise. The actress, however, was a no-show at the awards ceremony that year, due to press commitments for her upcoming movie X-Men: Apocalypse.

ACTOR WITH THE MOST
JIM MTV Movie Awards CARREY

Jim Carrey has eleven MTV Movie Awards, including five Best Comedic Performance awards for his roles in *Dumb and Dumber* (1994), *Ace Ventura: When Nature Calls* (1995), *The Cable Guy* (1996), *Liar Liar* (1997), and *Yes Man* (2008). He won the Best Villain award twice, once for *The Cable Guy* (1996) and the second time for *Dr. Seuss' How the Grinch Stole Christmas* (2000). Fans also awarded Carrey with the Best Kiss award for his lip-lock with Lauren Holly in *Dumb and Dumber*.

ACTORS WITH THE MOST MTV MOVIE AWARDS

⭐⭐⭐⭐⭐ **Jim Carrey 11**

⭐⭐⭐⭐ **Robert Pattinson 10**

⭐⭐⭐ **Mike Myers 7**

⭐⭐ **Adam Sandler 6**

⭐⭐ **Will Smith 6**

TOP-EARNING
actress
EMMA STONE

Arizona-born Emma Stone was the top-earning actress of 2017, with an income of $26 million. In the same year, she won an Oscar for her role in the musical *La La Land*, in which she plays a wannabe Hollywood actress who meets and falls in love with a jazz pianist played by Ryan Gosling—also nominated for an Oscar for his role. Stone beat two Jennifers—Aniston and Lawrence—to claim the title; Jennifer Lawrence, holder of the title in 2015 and 2016, was third on the list, while Jennifer Aniston came in second.

TOP-EARNING ACTRESSES 2017
In millions of U.S. dollars

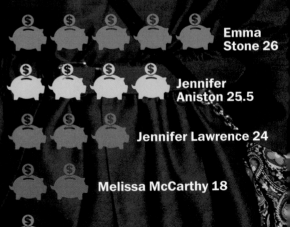

Emma Stone 26

Jennifer Aniston 25.5

Jennifer Lawrence 24

Melissa McCarthy 18

Mila Kunis 15.5

TOP-EARNING actor MARK WAHLBERG

Mark Wahlberg earned a colossal $68 million in 2017. The Boston-born actor starred in the hit movies *Daddy's Home 2* and *Transformers: The Last Knight*, which grossed $786 million combined worldwide. He also earned money as a spokesperson for AT&T. That's not all that keeps Mark Wahlberg busy—and wealthy. He has his own nationwide string of burger restaurants and stars alongside members of his family in the reality show *Wahlbergers*.

TOP-EARNING ACTORS 2017
In millions of U.S. dollars

Mark Wahlberg 68

Dwayne "The Rock" Johnson 65

Vin Diesel 54.5

Adam Sandler 50.5

Jackie Chan 49

TOP-GROSSING
movie
STAR WARS EPISODE VIII: THE LAST JEDI

Amassing more than fifty-seven million ticket sales in total, *Star Wars Episode VIII: The Last Jedi* was America's top-earning movie of 2017. The film grossed $517,218,368 in total—no mean feat, given that the film was not released until December 15. Directed by Rian Johnson, the movie continues the story set in *Star Wars: Episode VII: The Force Awakens*, released in 2015. Both films featured Carrie Fisher as Princess Leia—a role she had played in the first three Star Wars movies. Fisher passed away after filming, and as the credits roll at the end of the movie, a dedication reads: "In loving memory of our princess, Carrie Fisher."

TOP-EARNING MOVIES 2017
Gross in millions of U.S. dollars

Star Wars: Episode VIII: The Last Jedi 517

Beauty and the Beast 504

Wonder Woman 413

Guardians of the Galaxy Vol. 2 390

Spider-Man: Homecoming 334

DESPICABLE ME

Following the hugely successful 2017 release of the third movie in the series, *Despicable Me 3*, and with a global total of $3.528 billion, Despicable Me became the world's highest-grossing animated franchise of all time. The 2015 spin-off *Minions* is the most profitable animated film in Universal Studios' history and was the highest-grossing film of the year, while *Despicable Me 3* and Oscar-nominated *Despicable Me 2* hit spot no. 2 in their respective years of release. Collectively the four movies beat the Shrek franchise's takings of $3.51 billion, a total that includes sales from the spin-off *Puss in Boots*.

Andrew Lloyd Webber's *The Phantom of the Opera* opened on Broadway in January 1988 and has been performed more than 12,500 times. The original London cast members Michael Crawford, Sarah Brightman, and Steve Barton reprised their roles on Broadway. The story, based on a novel written in 1911 by French author Gaston Leroux, tells the tragic tale of the phantom and his love for an opera singer, Christine.

LONGEST-RUNNING Broadway show
THE PHANTOM OF THE OPERA

LONGEST-RUNNING BROADWAY SHOWS
Total performances (as of March 2018)

The Phantom of the Opera **12,526**

Chicago (1996 revival) **8,851**

The Lion King **8,453**

Cats **7,485**

Les Misérables **6,680**

HIGHEST-GROSSING
Broadway musical
THE LION KING

Since opening on November 13, 1997, *The Lion King* has earned $1.43 billion. The show is Broadway's third-longest-running production. *The Lion King* stage show is an adaptation of the hugely popular Disney animated film. Along with hit songs from the movie such as "Circle of Life" and "Hakuna Matata," the show includes new compositions by South African composer Lebo M. and others. The Broadway show features songs in six African languages, including Swahili and Congolese. Since it opened, *The Lion King* has attracted audiences totaling over eighty million people.

MUSICAL WITH THE MOST Tony Award nominations
HAMILTON

Lin-Manuel Miranda's musical biography of Founding Father Alexander Hamilton racked up an amazing sixteen Tony Award nominations to unseat the previous record holders, *The Producers* and *Billy Elliot the Musical*, both of which had fifteen. The mega-hit hip-hop musical, which was inspired by historian Ron Chernow's biography of the first secretary of the treasury, portrays the Founding Fathers of the United States engaging in rap battles over issues such as the national debt and the French Revolution. *Hamilton* won eleven Tonys at the 2016 ceremony—one shy of *The Producers*, which retains the record for most Tony wins with twelve. *Hamilton*'s Broadway success paved the way for the show to open in Chicago in 2016, with a touring show and a London production following in 2017.

YOUNGEST WINNER
of a Laurence Olivier Award

In 2012, four actresses shared an Olivier Award for their roles in the British production of *Matilda*. Eleanor Worthington-Cox, Cleo Demetriou, Kerry Ingram, and Sophia Kiely all won the award for Best Actress in a Musical. Of the four actresses, Worthington-Cox, age ten, was the youngest by a few weeks. Each actress portraying Matilda performs two shows a week. In the U.S., the four *Matilda* actresses won a special Tony Honors for Excellence in the Theatre in 2013. *Matilda*, inspired by the book by Roald Dahl, won a record seven Olivier Awards in 2012.

ELEANOR
WORTHINGTON-COX

CLEO
DEMETRIOU

KERRY
INGRAM

SOPHIA
KIELY

3

on the MOVE

ON THE MOVE
TRENDING#

BRAVO FOR JUNO
Jupiter space probe

2017 marked the first full year of NASA's *Juno* spacecraft mission, and the probe is currently in orbit around the planet Jupiter. It has been sending images and data back to Earth since arriving in July 2016, and will continue to do so until July 2021. In July 2017, *Juno* made its first pass over Jupiter's Great Red Spot—a mass of stormy clouds that is 1.3 times as wide as planet Earth.

MARVEL PLUG
Spider-Man drives an Audi

Audi's latest collaboration with Marvel Comics and Sony Pictures was an online ad featuring British actor Tom Holland in his new role as Spider-Man in 2017. Launched to coincide with the release date of *Spider-Man: Homecoming*—and announcing the new 2018 Audi   A8 —the ad told the story of Holland's character taking his driver's license test. During the course of the ad, the boy demonstrates features of the car's driver-assistance technology and even foils a bank heist while his examiner chats away in the passenger seat. A resounding success, the ad was Audi's most liked content ever on YouTube with 159,000 likes.

SPEED DEMON
World's fastest bumper car

As a challenge for TV show *Top Gear*, engineer Colin Furze created a world record–breaking bumper car capable of hitting speeds of over 100 miles per hour (twenty times faster than usual). Tested on the track by the show's anonymous racing driver, the Stig, the fairground favorite hit 100.336 miles per hour to claim the Guinness title.

TEAM ZAMBONI
Working the ice at the Winter Olympics

The 2018 Winter Olympics in Pyeongchang, South Korea, saw a different kind of team at play—the Zamboni drivers. Mostly U.S. and Canadian drivers, these ice technicians had the important job of keeping the ice in tip-top condition. Zamboni is the brand name of the big machines that make the ice smooth as they ride back and forth and round and round to resurface rinks and tracks all over the world.

SPOOF CAR AD
Viral car commercial

In November 2017, used-car retail giant CarMax paid out $20,000 for a 1996 Honda Accord that had 141,095 miles on the clock and an asking price of just $499. This bizarre event was the outcome of a used-car commercial that went viral days after being posted on YouTube. Created by filmmaker Max Lanman, and touching the hearts of many, the ad was a spoof on professional ads and tracked the car as it toured California's coastal landscape.

WORLD'S first MONSTER SCHOOL BUS

"Bad to the Bone" is the first monster school bus in the world. This revamped 1956 yellow bus is 13 feet tall, thanks to massive tires with 25-inch rims. The oversize bus weighs 19,000 pounds and is a favorite ride at charity events in California. But don't expect to get anywhere in a hurry—this "Kool Bus" is not built for speed and goes at a maximum of just 7 miles per hour.

street-legal car
KOENIGSEGG CCXR TREVITA

Costing $4.8 million, the Koenigsegg CCXR Trevita is one of the world's most exclusive cars. Koenigsegg, a Swedish manufacturer, built only two Trevitas. One of the vehicle's unique features is the specially created silvery-white, carbon-weave bodywork. In bright light, the finish looks as if it contains millions of tiny white diamonds. It also gives the car its name: *Trevita* means "three whites" in Swedish. At top speed, the hypercar can hit 254 miles per hour, and it can reach 62 miles per hour in under three seconds.

MOST EXPENSIVE CARS
(as of 2016) In U.S. dollars

Koenigsegg CCXR Trevita
4.8 million

$$$$

Lamborghini Veneno
4.5 million

$$$$

McLaren P1 LM
3.6 million

$$$$

Mansory Vivere Bugatti Veyron
3.4 million

$$$$

W Motors Lykan HyperSport
3.4 million

$$$$

BIGGEST monster truck BIGFOOT

Standing 15 feet 6 inches tall and weighing 38,000 pounds, Bigfoot #5 is the king of monster trucks. Bob Chandler purchased a Ford pickup truck in 1974 and began creating the first Bigfoot monster truck in 1975. In 1986, Chandler introduced Bigfoot #5, the largest ever. The truck's tires are 10 feet tall and come from an Alaskan land train used by the U.S. Army in the 1950s. Chandler built over a dozen more Bigfoot trucks, but none of these newbies matches the size of Bigfoot #5.

SMALLEST trailer
QTVAN

The tiny QTvan is just over 7 feet long, 2.5 feet wide, and 5 feet tall. Inside, however, it has a full-size single bed, a kettle for boiling water, and a 19-inch TV. The Environmental Transport Association (ETA) in Britain sponsored the invention of the minitrailer, which was designed to be pulled by a mobility scooter. The ETA recommends the QTvan for short trips only, since mobility scooters have a top speed of 6 miles per hour, at best.

FASTEST land vehicle

THRUST SSC

The world's fastest car is the Thrust SSC, which reached a speed of 763 miles per hour on October 15, 1997, in the Black Rock Desert, Nevada. *SSC* stands for supersonic (faster than the speed of sound). The Thrust SSC's amazing speed comes from two jet engines with 110,000 brake horsepower. That's as much as 145 Formula One race cars. The British-made car uses about 5 gallons of jet fuel in one second and takes just five seconds to reach its top speed. At that speed, the Thrust SSC could travel from New York City to San Francisco in less than four hours. More recently, another British manufacturer has developed a new supersonic car, the Bloodhound, with a projected speed of 1,000 miles per hour. If it reaches that, it will set a new world record.

60

In September 2017, the high-speed rail service between Beijing and Shanghai started using new Fuxing Hao bullet trains. With an operating speed of 220 miles per hour, it is the fastest passenger train in the world. According to figures from the rail operator, China Railway, about 600 million passengers use the Beijing-Shanghai line each year. Other high-speed trains, such as Japan's SCMaglev and France's TGV may have reached higher speeds in testing (375 and 357 miles per hour respectively, compared to Fuxing's 250 miles per hour), but both are capped at 200 miles per hour when it comes to carrying passengers.

FASTEST PASSENGER TRAINS
(maximum operating speed)

China Fuxing Hao 220 mph

Japan SCMaglev 200 mph

France TGV 200 mph

Spain AVE 200 mph

German ICE 200 mph

FASTEST
passenger train
FUXING
HAO

In June 2016, World Supersport rider Kenan Sofuoğlu set a new land-speed record for a production motorcycle—that is, a mass-produced, road-worthy, two-wheeled motorcycle. He reached a top speed of 249 miles per hour in just twenty-six seconds. He was riding the Kawasaki Ninja H2R, currently the fastest production motorcycle in the world, while crossing the Osman Gazi Bridge in Turkey. At 8,799 feet across, this is the world's fourth-longest suspension bridge. The Ninja H2R is currently legal for track racing only, and while Kawasaki produces a street-legal Ninja, it is not the world's fastest. That honor goes to the Madmax Streetfighter, which has a top speed of 233 miles per hour.

FASTEST production motorcycle

KAWASAKI NINJA H2R

LARGEST cruise ship ROYAL CARIBBEAN
Symphony of the Seas

With a gross tonnage of 230,000 tons, the new Royal Caribbean cruise ship *Symphony of the Seas* now holds the record for the world's largest. It beats last year's record holder, the 226,963-GT *Harmony of the Seas*, also a Royal Caribbean ship. *Symphony of the Seas* has 2,774 cabins and can carry 5,535 guests at full capacity. The two-story Ultimate Family Suite has an air-hockey table, a LEGO® climbing wall, and a private 3-D movie room with a library of video games and its own popcorn machine.

WORLD'S LARGEST CRUISE SHIPS
Gross tonnage (in tons)

Symphony of the Seas,
Royal Caribbean 230,000

Harmony of the Seas, **Royal Caribbean 226,963**

Allure of the Seas, **Royal Caribbean 225,282**

Oasis of the Seas, **Royal Caribbean 225,282**

MSC Meraviglia **171,598**

FASTEST
helicopter circumnavigation of Earth

JENNIFER MURRAY AND COLIN BODILL

In 2007, British pilots Jennifer Murray and Colin Bodill became the first pilots ever to fly around the world in a helicopter via the North and South Poles. They also set the record for the fastest time to complete this journey, at 170 days, 22 hours, 47 minutes, and 17 seconds. The pair began and ended their record-setting journey in Fort Worth, Texas, and flew a Bell 407 helicopter. The journey, which began on December 5, 2006, and ended on May 23, 2007, was the duo's second attempt at the record. The first, in 2003, ended with an emergency rescue after they crashed in Antarctica.

LIGHTEST jet BD-5J MICROJET

In 2004, the BD-5J Microjet, a one-seater aircraft, secured the record as the world's lightest jet. The jet weighs 358.8 pounds, has a 17-foot wingspan, and is only 12 feet long. Engineer Jim Bede introduced the microjet in the early 1970s and sold hundreds in kit form, ready for self-assembly. The BD-5J model became a popular airshow attraction and was featured in a James Bond movie. The microjet uses a TRS-18 turbojet engine and can carry only 32 gallons of fuel. Its top speed is 300 miles per hour.

FASTEST
unmanned plane X-43A

In November 2004, NASA launched its experimental X-43A plane for a test flight over the Pacific Ocean. The X-43A plane reached Mach 9.6, which is more than nine times the speed of sound and nearly 7,000 miles per hour. A B-52B aircraft carried the X-43A and a Pegasus rocket booster into the air, releasing them at 40,000 feet. At that point, the booster—essentially a fuel-packed engine—ignited, blasting the unmanned X-43A higher and faster, before separating from the plane. The plane continued to fly for several minutes at 110,000 feet, before crashing (intentionally) into the ocean.

NASA

1 X-43A

HELIOS 1 AND HELIOS 2

TITAN/CENTAUR

Helios 1 and *Helios 2* are space probes launched in the 1970s to orbit the sun. A probe, equipped with cameras, sensors, and computers, can transmit information back to Earth. Both probes are extremely fast, with *Helios 2* reaching 153,800 miles per hour. *Helios 2* flew closest to the sun, getting within 32 million miles from the center of the enormous star. It takes the probes about 190 days to orbit the sun. In 2018, NASA plans to send another probe, Parker Solar Probe, which will go even closer to the sun. This probe could hit speeds as high as 450,000 miles per hour.

67

APOLLO 10 FLIGHT STATS

05/18/69
LAUNCH DATE: May 18, 1969

12:49
LAUNCH TIME: 12:49 p.m. EDT

05/21/69
ENTERED LUNAR ORBIT: May 21, 1969

192:03:23
DURATION OF MISSION: 192 hours, 3 minutes, 23 seconds

05/26/69
RETURN DATE: May 26, 1969

12:52
SPLASHDOWN: 12:52 p.m. EDT

manned spacecraft

APOLLO 10

NASA's *Apollo 10* spacecraft reached its top speed on its descent to Earth, hurtling through the atmosphere at 24,816 miles per hour and splashing down on May 26, 1969. The spacecraft's crew had traveled faster than anyone on Earth. The mission was a "dress rehearsal" for the first moon landing by *Apollo 11*, two months later. The *Apollo 10* spacecraft consisted of a Command Service Module, called Charlie Brown, and a Lunar Module, called Snoopy. Today, Charlie Brown is on display at the Science Museum in London, England.

LIFT-OFF
The *Apollo 10* spacecraft was launched from Cape Canaveral, known as Cape Kennedy at the time. It was the fourth manned Apollo launch in seven months.

FASTEST
roller coaster
FORMULA ROSSA

FASTEST ROLLER COASTERS

 **Formula Rossa, Abu Dhabi, UAE 149.1 mph**

 Kingda Ka, New Jersey, USA 128 mph

Top Thrill Dragster, Ohio, USA 120 mph

Dodonpa, Yamanashi, Japan 112 mph

 Red Force, Ferrari Land, Tarragona, Spain 112 mph

FORMULA ROSSA
World Records
Speed: 149.1 mph
G-force: 1.7 Gs
Acceleration: 4.8 Gs

Thrill seekers hurtle along the Formula Rossa track at 149.1 miles per hour. The high-speed roller coaster is part of Ferrari World in Abu Dhabi, United Arab Emirates. Ferrari World also features the world's largest indoor theme park, at 925,696 square miles. The Formula Rossa roller coaster seats are red Ferrari-shaped cars that travel from 0 to 62 miles per hour in just two seconds—as fast as a race car. The ride's G-force is so extreme that passengers must wear goggles to protect their eyes. G-force acts on a body due to acceleration and gravity. People can withstand 6 to 8 Gs for short periods. The Formula Rossa G-Force is 4.8 Gs during acceleration and 1.7 Gs at maximum speed.

TALLEST
water
coaster

MASSIV

Schlitterbahn Galveston Island Waterpark in Texas is home to the world's tallest water coaster—the aptly named MASSIV, measures in at 81 feet and 6.72 inches tall. A water coaster is a water slide that features ascents as well as descents, with riders traveling in rafts or tubes. MASSIV, which the park calls a "monster blaster," was built for the tenth anniversary of the opening of Schlitterbahn Galveston. Riders sit in two-person tubes, which take them over a series of dips and four uphill climbs before dropping into the final landing pool. In April 2016, the park released a virtual version of the ride, allowing people all over the world to see MASSIV from the point of view of a rider.

CIRCUS

OLDEST
merry-go-round
FLYING HORSES CAROUSEL

Taking a spin around the Flying Horses Carousel in Martha's Vineyard is a trip back in time. Charles Dare constructed the carousel in 1876 for an amusement park in Coney Island, New York. The carousel moved to Oak Bluffs, Massachusetts, in 1884. A preservation society took over Flying Horses in 1986 to restore the carousel and keep it intact and working. Today, the horses look just as colorful as they did in the 1800s. Their manes are real horsehair, and they have glass eyes. As the horses turn around and around, a 1923 Wurlitzer Band Organ plays old-time music. The Flying Horses Carousel is a National Landmark.

LARGEST
tunnel-boring machine
BERTHA

In July 2013, Bertha started drilling out a 2-mile-long tunnel beneath Seattle, Washington. Bertha is a tunnel-boring machine built in Japan at a cost of $80 million. She weighs 7,000 tons and, at 300 feet long, she is almost the length of a football field. The machine's massive cutting head alone is 57.5 feet in diameter

and consists of a steel face and 600 cutting disks. In December 2013, Bertha stopped working. The crew dug an access pit to retrieve her cutting head for repairs. In December 2015, Bertha resumed her work. The machine's fans follow Bertha's progress on her Twitter page. At one point she had 72,000 followers.

super STRUCTURES

SUPER STRUCTURES
TRENDING

CULTURAL HIT
#TheLouvre

The Louvre museum in Paris was ranked as the most Instagrammed art museum of 2017, beating out New York's Metropolitan Museum of Art and Museum of Modern Art, and London's British Museum, among others. Boasting 8.1 million visitors in 2017, the Louvre is the largest art museum in the world. It houses about 38,000 artifacts in total—the most famous of which is Leonardo da Vinci's *Mona Lisa*.

AMAZON SPHERES
A workplace in the jungle

Three lush, plant-filled, steel-and-glass spheres opened in Seattle, Washington, in January 2018, the newest addition to Amazon's growing enterprise. The domes are filled with plant species from across the globe, and include a "living wall" that starts on the ground floor and extends through all four stories of the central dome. Kept at a steady 72 degrees Fahrenheit during the day, the domes offer up to 800 employees a junglelike environment in which to hold meetings and socialize.

FROM HIGHWAY TO SKYWAY
Seoullo 7017

Seoul, South Korea, is leading a trend in massive urban gardens, having transformed an inner-city overpass into a stunning public walkway. Measuring more than 100,000 square feet, the garden is planted with 24,000 trees, shrubs, and flowers. Seasonal changes ensure year-round color and perfume. The skyway's Korean name, *Seoullo*, translates as "Seoul Street," and 7017 stands for two significant years in its history: 1970—the year of the bypass's original construction, and 2017—when it was completed as this greener, more attractive space.

DOWNSIZING
The growing fashion for tiny houses

Architects trying to limit the impact that buildings have on the environment are making homes smaller. One of the smallest of 2017 is a house in London that measures just 140 square feet. Architects at the firm Studiomama (pictured) have made clever use of custom-made units to make the space—which includes a fold-up bed, fold-out seating, and a stand-up desk—as multifunctional as possible.

DOORS OPENING
Revolutionary elevator system

In 2017 German company Thyssenkrupp Elevator revealed an elevator that moves sideways. The technology relies on the same kind of magnetic levitation used by high-speed trains. It means that elevators of the future will be able to move up, down, and sideways. It will be a couple of years before we see Thyssenkrupp's first sideways elevator in action—it's due for installation in a building in Berlin, Germany, in 2021.

CITY WITH THE MOST
skyscrapers in the world
HONG KONG

Hong Kong, China, has 317 buildings that reach 500 feet or higher, and three more under construction. Six are 980 feet or higher. The tallest three are the International Commerce Centre (ICC) at 1,588 feet; Two International Finance Centre at 1,352 feet; and Central Plaza at 1,227 feet. Hong Kong's stunning skyline towers above Victoria Harbour. Most of its tallest buildings are on Hong Kong Island, although the other side of the harbor, Kowloon, is growing. Every night a light, laser, and sound show called "A Symphony of Lights" illuminates the sky against a backdrop of some forty of Hong Kong's skyscrapers.

CITIES WITH THE MOST SKYSCRAPERS IN THE WORLD
Number of skyscrapers at 500 feet or higher

Hong Kong, China 317

New York City, USA 251

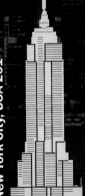

Dubai, UAE 156

Tokyo, Japan 143

LARGEST
sports stadium
RUNGRADO MAY FIRST STADIUM

It took over two years to build Rungrado May First Stadium, a gigantic sports venue that seats up to 150,000 people. The 197-foot-tall stadium opened in 1989 on Rungra Island in North Korea's capital, Pyongyang. The stadium hosts international soccer matches on its natural grass pitch, and has other facilities such as an indoor swimming pool, training halls, and a 1,312-foot rubberized running track. The annual gymnastics and artistic festival Arirang also takes place here.

LARGEST SPORTS STADIUMS
By capacity

Rungrado May First Stadium, North Korea 150,000

Michigan Stadium, Michigan, USA 107,601

Beaver Stadium, Pennsylvania, USA 107,282

Estadio Azteca, Mexico 105,064

AT&T Stadium, Texas, USA 105,000

LARGEST
home in an airliner
727
BOEING

Bruce Campbell's home is not that large, but it is the biggest of its kind. Campbell lives in 1,066 square feet within a grounded 727 Boeing airplane. The airplane no longer has an engine, but Campbell kept the cockpit and its original instruments. He also installed a transparent floor to make the structure of the plane visible. The retired engineer purchased the plane for $100,000 and paid for its transportation to his property in Oregon. Now trees surround the plane instead of sky. Visitors are welcome to take a tour.

LARGEST
house shaped like a VW beetle
VOGLREITER RESIDENCE

Architect Markus Voglreiter turned an ordinary home in Gnigl, near Salzburg, Austria, into an attention-grabbing showpiece: a Volkswagen Beetle–shaped house. The eco-friendly home, completed in 2003, is energy efficient and offers separate, comfortable living quarters. The car-shaped extension measures 950 square feet and is over 32 feet tall. At night, two of the home's windows look like car headlights.

Just one night at Geneva's Hotel President Wilson could set you back $80,000. That is the going rate for the hotel's Royal Penthouse Suite, making it the most expensive hotel in the world. At 18,083 square feet, the suite is also Europe's largest. Occupying the entire eighth floor of the hotel, the Royal Penthouse Suite has terraces overlooking Lake Geneva and rooms for up to twelve guests. Luxury amenities include a private gym, a telescope for stargazing at night, a Steinway grand piano, a billiard table, and a collection of antique books. Since guests include top celebrities and heads of state, the suite naturally comes with maximum-security features, such as a private elevator, a reinforced safe, and bulletproof glass.

WORLD'S MOST
expensive hotel
HOTEL PRESIDENT WILSON, SWITZERLAND

hotel made of salt
PALACIO DE SAL

Hotel Palacio de Sal in Uyuni, Bolivia, is the first hotel in the world made completely out of salt. Originally built in 1998, construction began on the new Palacio de Sal hotel in 2004. The hotel overlooks the biggest salt flat in the world, Salar de Uyuni, which covers 4,086 square miles. Builders used around one million blocks of salt to create the hotel walls, floors, ceilings, and furniture. Some of the hotel's thirty rooms have igloo-shaped roofs. The salt flats lie in an area once covered by Lago Minchin, an ancient salt lake. When the lake dried up, it left salt pans, one of which was the Salar de Uyuni.

ANOTHER STRANGE PLACE TO STAY

Hotel shaped like a dog: Dog Bark Park Inn in Cottonwood, Idaho, where you can sleep inside a wooden beagle that measures 33 feet tall and 16 feet wide.

DUBAI'S BURJ KHALIFA
WORLD RECORDS:
Tallest building: 2,717 feet
Most floors: 160
Fastest elevators: 55 feet per second

Laid end to end, the
steel used here would
stretch one-quarter of the way around the world!

WORLD'S TALLEST building

BURJ KHALIFA

IT CAN SWAY UP TO 3.9 FEET!

GOING UP!
THE UPPER SECTION IS STEEL FRAMED, SO IT'S POSSIBLE TO MAKE IT TALLER. DURING BUILDING, ITS HEIGHT WAS RAISED THREE TIMES.

LARGEST
freestanding
building
NEW
CENTURY
GLOBAL
CENTER

The New Century Global Center in Chengdu, southwestern China, is an enormous 18.9 million square feet. That's nearly three times the size of the U.S. Pentagon. Completed in 2013, the structure is 328 feet tall, 1,640 feet long, and 1,312 feet deep. The multiuse building houses a 4.3-million-square-foot shopping mall, two hotels, an Olympic-size ice rink, a fourteen-screen IMAX cinema complex, and offices. It even has its own Paradise Island, a beach resort complete with artificial sun.

swimming pool LARGEST
CITYSTARS POOL

The Citystars lagoon in Sharm el-Sheikh, Egypt, stretches over 30 acres. It was created by Crystal Lagoons, the same company that built the former record holder at San Alfonso del Mar in Chile. The lagoon at Sharm el-Sheikh cost $5.5 million to create and is designed to be sustainable, using salt water from local underground aquifers. The creators purify this water not just for recreation, but also to provide clean, fresh water to the surrounding community.

LARGEST SWIMMING POOLS
Size in acres

Citystars, Egypt 30

San Alfonso del Mar, Chile 19.7

Ocean Dome, Japan 7.4

Dead Sea, China 7.4

Orthlieb Pool, Morocco 3.7

TALLEST
tree house
THE MINISTER'S HOUSE

Minister **Horace** Burgess began building his **tree** house in 1993, and took many years erecting the towering, ten-story, 97-foot-high structure. **The** main support is an 80-foot-tall white **oak** tree, while six other trees provide reinforcement. The Minister's House, as it is known, is in a wooded area in Crossville, Tennessee, and includes a church topped by a chime **tower**. Thousands came to visit the amazing attraction every year, until the **State** Fire Marshal temporarily **closed** the **tree** house in 2012 due **to fire** hazards.

WORLD'S greenest city
SINGAPORE

According to a new study from Treepedia, Singapore has the highest percentage of urban greenery in the world. Treepedia is the work of the Senseable City Laboratory at Massachusetts Institute of Technology (MIT). By analyzing panoramas posted on Google Street View, the Treepedia program assesses the level of vegetation in a city and rates it on a scale of 0–100 in its Green View Index (GVI). The program shows the real level of greenery in the streets on which city people live and work. The people behind Treepedia hope to raise greater awareness in cities in which trees are lacking, and to encourage developers to include them in future projects.

GREENEST CITIES
Treepedia's GVI rating

🌳 🌳 🌳 🌳 🌳 **Singapore 29.3%**

🌳 🌳 🌳 🌳 **Sydney, Australia 25.9%**

🌳 🌳 🌳 **Vancouver, Canada 25.9%**

🌳 🌳 **Cambridge, MA, USA 25.3%**

🌳 **Durban, South Africa 23.7%**

LARGEST
vertical garden
KAOHSIUNG
CITY

A vertical garden in Kaohsiung City, Taiwan, is the largest in the world at 27,922 square feet, almost the size of ten tennis courts! The garden, also called a "green wall," was completed in June 2015 and forms part of a fence around Cleanaway Company Ltd., a waste-disposal company. Construction took about two months and more than 100,000 plants. From afar, the panorama shows a landscape at sunset, with a bright red sun. However, green walls are not only beautiful; they help to lower pollution and CO_2 emissions.

WORLD'S LARGEST
greenhouse
EDEN PROJECT

COUNTRY WITH THE MOST GREENHOUSES

The Netherlands: Greenhouses cover more than 25 square miles of the country's entire area.

The Eden Project sprawls over 32 acres of land in the countryside of Cornwall, England. Nestled in the cavity of an old clay pit mine, it's the world's largest greenhouse and has been open since 2003. Eight interlinked, transparent domes house two distinct biomes. The first is a rain forest region and the second is Mediterranean. Each has around one thousand plant varieties. Visitors can see a further three thousand different plants in the 20 acres of outdoor gardens. During construction, the Eden Project used a record-breaking 230 miles of scaffolding.

LARGEST
tomb of a known individual
QIN SHI HUANG'S TOMB

FIRST EMPEROR OF CHINA
Emperor Qin Shi Huang was the first emperor of a unified China. Before his rule, the territory had been a collection of independent states. He was just forty-nine years old when he died.

QIN SHI HUANG'S TOMB STATS

1974
YEAR OF DISCOVERY: 1974

36
NUMBER OF YEARS IT TOOK TO CREATE: 36

8,000
TOTAL NUMBER OF FIGURES FOUND: 8,000

221–207
DURATION OF THE QIN DYNASTY: 221–207 BCE

Emperor Qin Shi Huang ruled China from 221 BCE to 207 BCE He is famous for uniting China's empire. In 1974, people digging a well in the fields northeast of Xi'an, in Shaanxi province, accidentally discovered the ancient tomb. Further investigation by archaeologists revealed a burial complex over 20 square miles. A large pit contained 6,000 life-size terra-cotta warrior figures, each one different from the next and dressed according to rank. A second and third pit contained 2,000 more figures, clay horses, about 40,000 bronze weapons, and other artifacts. Historians think that 700,000 people worked for about thirty-six years to create this incredible mausoleum. The emperor's tomb remains sealed to preserve its contents and to protect workers from possible hazards, such as chemical poisoning from mercury in the surrounding soil.

LARGEST
castle
PRAGUE CASTLE

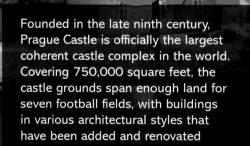

Founded in the late ninth century, Prague Castle is officially the largest coherent castle complex in the world. Covering 750,000 square feet, the castle grounds span enough land for seven football fields, with buildings in various architectural styles that have been added and renovated throughout the centuries. Formerly the home of kings and empresses, the castle is now occupied by the president of the Czech Republic and his family, and is also open to tourists. The palace contains four churches, including the famous St. Vitus Cathedral.

LARGEST
sand
castle

DUISBURG, GERMANY

On September 1, 2017, German tour operator and travel agency Schauinsland-Reisen GmbH built a sand castle measuring 54 feet 9 inches—the tallest ever recorded—in the city of Duisburg. The team that created the sand castle spent almost a month doing so, using around 3,850 metric tons of sand that had been delivered by 168 trucks.

The design of the sand castle includes some of the most famous tourist spots across the globe, including the Leaning Tower of Pisa and the Acropolis in Athens. Measured using laser technology, the sand castle was half a foot taller than that of the previous record set on the beach at Puri, Odisha, India, just seven months earlier.

OMER TOWER
TEL AVIV, ISRAEL
RECORD-BREAKING
LEGO® tower

During the last few weeks of December 2017, a LEGO® tower measuring 117 feet and 11 inches tall was built in Rabin Square, Tel Aviv. Several thousand volunteers came together to build the sky-high monument in memory of Omer Sayag, an eight-year-old boy who died of cancer in 2014. Tel Aviv City Hall worked with Young Engineers, an organization that promotes learning through building with toy bricks. They used over half a million LEGO® bricks in total. Once complete, it broke the record for the tallest-ever LEGO® tower, beating the previous record of 116 feet, 4 inches, set in Günzberg, Germany, in June 2016, by 19 inches.

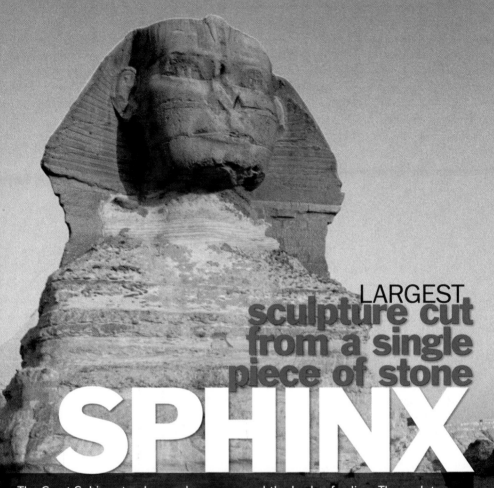

LARGEST
sculpture cut from a single piece of stone
SPHINX

The Great Sphinx stands guard near three large pyramids at Giza, Egypt. Historians believe that ancient people created the gigantic sculpture about 4,500 years ago for the pharaoh Khafre. They carved the sphinx from one mass of limestone in the desert floor, creating a sculpture about 66 feet high and 240 feet long. It has the head of a pharaoh and the body of a lion. The sculpture may represent Ruti, a twin lion god from ancient myths that protected the sun god, Ra, and guarded entrances to the underworld. Sand has covered and preserved the Great Sphinx, but over many years, wind and humidity have worn parts of the soft limestone away, some of which have been restored using blocks.

GREAT SPHINX FACTS
Age: 4,500 years (estimated)
Length: 240 ft
Height: 66 ft

5

high
TECH

HIGH TECH
TRENDING

SPIN LIKE CRAZY!
The year of the fidget spinner

Fidget spinners took the world by storm in 2017. The palm-size, three-armed, plastic or metal toys have a ball bearing at their center and spin for minutes if balanced correctly on the finger. The toys proved so popular that, at one point, Toys "R" Us were said to be using chartered jets to keep their shelves well enough stocked to meet demand.

NOT HEROES BUT SHEROES
Barbie's inspirational women

Barbie celebrated International Women's Day on March 8, 2018, with the launch of two new series of dolls based on real-life women. The Sheroes and Inspiring Women honor fourteen present-day and three historic women who have been influential in their spheres, whether cultural, scientific, sport, or business-related. The role models include artist Frida Kahlo, conservationist Bindi Irwin, principal ballerina Misty Copeland, and film director Ava DuVernay.

LEGO® PIECES GO GREEN
Sustainable LEGO® parts

The LEGO® Group announced a neat new directive in March 2018. From now on, all its plantlike model pieces—trees, bushes, and leaves—will be made using plastic derived from plant-based materials, namely sugarcane. The move is part of the LEGO® Group's bid to reduce damage to the environment by making sustainable parts for its kits. The company hopes to make the majority of its products and packaging from sustainable materials by 2030.

DOWNHILL ALL THE WAY
Ski Robot Challenge

Not far from the 2017 Winter Olympics site in Pyeongchang, South Korea, eight robots took up the challenge of winning $10,000 for their teams in the Ski Robot Challenge. Points were awarded for navigating a slalom without hitting too many flagpoles and crossing the line in the fastest time. At just 29.5 inches tall, Taekwon V won gold for its team Minirobot Corp, completing the course in just eighteen seconds.

NUGGS FOR CARTER
The ultimate teen dream

A sixteen-year-old from Reno, Nevada, made Twitter history in 2017 by breaking the record for the most Retweeted Tweet. Carter Wilkerson's Tweet read: "Help me please. A man needs his nuggs." He was rising to a challenge set by Wendy's—18 million Retweets and a year's supply of chicken nuggets would be his. By April 2018, Carter had 3.7 million Retweets and Wendy's agreed it was enough to earn Carter his nuggets.

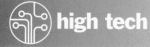

CELEBRITY WITH THE MOST Instagram followers
SELENA GOMEZ

CELEBRITIES WITH THE MOST INSTAGRAM FOLLOWERS 2017
In millions of followers

- Selena Gomez 130
- Cristiano Ronaldo 116
- Ariana Grande 115
- Beyoncé 108
- **Kim Kardashian West 104**

Singer and former Disney Channel star Selena Gomez reached 130 million Instagram followers in 2017, holding on to her title as the most popular celebrity Instagrammer for the second year running. She also claimed five out of the top ten most-liked Instagram posts of the year. One included a dedication to Francia Raisa, who donated a kidney to Gomez in 2017. Since 2015, the star had been suffering from lupus, a disease that causes the immune system to attack healthy body parts, and needed a kidney transplant.

MOST RETWEETED
photo ever
ELLEN DEGENERES

Ellen DeGeneres's selfie taken at the 2014 Oscars is the most Retweeted photo ever. The photo, which pictures DeGeneres, Bradley Cooper, Jennifer Lawrence, and many other celebrities, has over 3.3 million Retweets. In just over one hour, the post was Retweeted more than 1 million times. The rush of activity on Twitter crashed the social networking site for a short time. Before the Oscar selfie took over Twitter, President Obama held the record for the most Retweeted photo. On November 6, 2012, the president posted an election victory photo and Tweet that has been Retweeted over 900,000 times.

TOP-GROSSING mobile game app
CANDY CRUSH SAGA

TOP-GROSSING MOBILE GAME APPS
Daily revenue in U.S. dollars (as of April 2018)

Candy Crush Saga 2,244,487

Candy Crush Soda Saga 1,682,662

Golf Clash 1,290,434

Clash Royale 1,014,965

Clash of Clans 885,805

The free online gaming app *Candy Crush Saga* had the highest daily revenue of all iPhone gaming apps in 2017. Gamers work their way through each level by switching colored candies to match them in rows of three. Configurations of four or five of the same color earn a player special candies to help clear the board more quickly. Players are given various tasks from one level to the next, such as clearing jelly or working within a set time limit. Although the game is free, players can buy boosters to complete hard and super-hard levels. That's how the game's developer, King, earns its money.

MOST VIEWED
YouTube
video ever
"DESPACITO"

In 2017, "Despacito"
by Luis Fonsi and Daddy
Yankee (later remixed by
Justin Bieber) became the world's
most viewed YouTube video ever. With
more than five billion views and counting, the video broke
the record on approaching the three billion mark in August
2017. The record knocked Wiz Khalifa and Charlie Puth's
"See You Again" from the top spot. "See You Again" had
only just taken the crown from Psy's "Gangnam Style."

MOST-USED
Instagram
hashtag

The most popular hashtag on Instagram in 2017 was used to caption a variety of photographs—romantic selfies, cute animals, even shots of new shoes. The picture-sharing platform displays more than 1.3 billion posts that use the tag #love, and the number continues to grow. Of the hashtags that increased in popularity in 2017, five out of ten are photography and travel related, with #photography and #travelphotography taking the top two spots.

#L😍VE

MOST POPULAR
beauty and style vlogger
YUYA

The Mexican vlogger Mariand Castrejón, aka Yuya, ranks as YouTube's most popular beauty vlogger based on channel subscriptions. When the ratings were taken in August 2017, Yuya had just over nineteen million subscribers, compared to the next highest in popularity, Zoella, with just under twelve million. According to Social Blade—YouTube's stats website—Yuya can make anywhere between $4,900 to $77,700 a month from her videos. The young woman started her channel in 2009 after winning a makeup video contest. Since that time she has posted numerous videos on women's beauty and has released her own line of makeup.

TOP BEAUTY AND STYLE VLOGGERS 2017
Subscribers in millions
(as of August 2017)

Yuya 19.19

Zoella 11.97

Bethany Mota 10.47

Michelle Phan 8.96

Rosanna Pansino 8.93

PRODUCT WITH THE MOST
Facebook fans
COCA-COLA

Soft drink giant Coca-Cola was again the most popular product on Facebook in 2017 with 107.4 million fans. The company posts photos, videos, and updates on its Timeline, while fans can post their own photos and questions for the company. Founded in 1886, Coca-Cola is now a multibillion-dollar enterprise, producing more than eighty drinks across twenty brands, including Evian, Oasis, and Minute Maid. The drinks sell in over 200 countries worldwide at a staggering rate of 1.9 billion servings per day.

PRODUCTS WITH THE MOST FACEBOOK FANS
In millions of fans, as of May 2018

 Coca-Cola 107.4

 Red Bull 49.0

 Nike Football 44.9

 Converse 44.2

 Oreo 43.2

PERSON WITH THE MOST
Facebook "likes"

Soccer pro Cristiano Ronaldo retained the top spot on Facebook in 2017 with over 122 million fans. Born in 1985, Ronaldo plays for both the Portuguese national team and Spanish powerhouse Real Madrid. As a teenager, Ronaldo's soccer skills were so impressive that British team Manchester United signed him for around $17 million. In 2008, Ronaldo earned the honor of FIFA World Player of the Year. The following year, Ronaldo transferred to Real Madrid for a record $115 million. In 2017, Ronaldo won the Ballon d'Or (Golden Ball) award for the fifth time.

PEOPLE WITH THE MOST FACEBOOK FANS
In millions of fans, as of May 2018

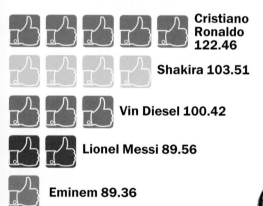

Cristiano Ronaldo 122.46

Shakira 103.51

Vin Diesel 100.42

Lionel Messi 89.56

Eminem 89.36

CRISTIANO RONALDO

DOG WITH THE MOST
Instagram followers JIFFPOM

On May 3, 2017, and with 4.8 million followers, Jiffpom broke the Guinness World Record for being the most popular dog on Instagram. Almost a year later, in April 2018, the dog's follower count had risen to 8.4 million. Jiffpom's owner posts snapshots of the fluffy little dog dressed in a wide range of cute outfits and Jiffpom even has a website. The Pomeranian from the United States has other records to boast of, too. At one time, he held the record for the fastest dog to cover a distance of 16.4 feet on his front legs (7.76 seconds). Another time, he was the record holder for covering 32.8 feet on his hind legs (6.56 seconds).

CAT WITH THE MOST Instagram followers
NALA CAT

With a total of 3.5 million followers, Nala Cat topped the bill as Instagram's most popular cat in 2017. Adopted from a shelter at just five months old, the Siamese-Tabby mix with bright blue eyes is now seven years old. Visitors to Nala's website can meet other members of her cat family—White Coffee, Stella and Steve, and Luna Rose. Fans can also track events in the cats' lives by reading Nala's blog.

GAME OF THE YEAR 2017

THE LEGEND OF ZELDA:

BREATH OF THE WILD

In February 2018, *The Legend of Zelda: Breath of the Wild* won Game of the Year at the twenty-first annual DICE awards, held in Las Vegas by the Academy of Interactive Arts and Sciences. The organization has more than 33,000 members and holds the event in celebration of the biggest achievements in video games

"DICE" stands for "Design, Innovate, Communicate, Entertain," and *Zelda* certainly managed to qualify in all of those categories, taking four awards in total. In addition to Game of the Year, *Breath of the Wild* won Adventure Game of the Year, Outstanding Achievement in Game Direction, and Outstanding Achievement in Game Design.

According to Newzoo, *League of Legends* was the most popular online game in 2017 and well into 2018. Ranking games by the number of unique players each month, *League of Legends* came out on top time and again. Riot Games created *League of Legends* in 2009, and it quickly became one of the most popular MOBA—Multiplayer Online Battle Arena—games. The game is free to play, although players purchase points to buy "champions," "boosts," and other virtual items to help them on the battlefield. The game is popular among eSports players, with teams competing in the *League of Legends* World Championship contests for big money.

MOST POPULAR
online game

LEAGUE OF LEGENDS

MOST POPULAR ONLINE GAMES
World ranking as of May 2018
1 *League of Legends*
2 *Hearthstone*
3 *Fortnite*
4 *PlayerUnknown's Battlegrounds*
5 *Counter-Strike: Global Offensive*

FASTEST-SELLING
gaming console

NINTENDO
SWITCH

Nintendo launched its new TV-handheld console in March 2017 and sold a whopping 906,000 units in the first month. That makes the Nintendo Switch the fastest-selling gaming console of the year. By the end of 2017, sales had risen to 14.86 million units, beating sales in the entire history of the company's sister console Wii U, which totaled 13.56 million units. The Nintendo Switch is a gaming console that you can plug into your TV to play at home, but that is also small enough to take out and about as a handheld console. Sales of games available for the console have been just as impressive, with *Super Mario Odyssey* selling nine million units, *Mario Kart 8* selling 7.3 million, and *The Legend of Zelda: Breath of the Wild* selling 6.7 million.

BESTSELLING
video game franchise of all time
MARIO

Nintendo's Mario franchise has sold 577 million units since the first game was released in 1981. Since then, Mario, his brother Luigi, and other characters like Princess Peach and Yoshi have become household names, starring in a number of games across consoles. In the early games, like *Super Mario World*, players jump over obstacles, collect tokens, and capture flags as Mario journeys through the Mushroom Kingdom to save the princess. The franchise has since diversified to include other popular games, such as *Mario Kart*, a racing game showcasing the inhabitants and landscapes of Mushroom Kingdom.

BESTSELLING VIDEO GAME FRANCHISES
Units sold in millions, as of March 2018

Mario (Nintendo)
577

Sonic the Hedgehog (Sega) 350

Pokémon (Game Freak) 295

Call of Duty (Infinity Ward) 250

Grand Theft Auto (Rockstar North) 220 million

MINEFAIRE STATS:

12,140

NUMBER OF PEOPLE ATTENDING
MINEFAIRE: 12,140

150,000

TOTAL AREA, IN SQUARE FEET,
OF *MINECRAFT*-CENTERED
ATTRACTIONS: 150,000

3

NUMBER OF GUINNESS WORLD
RECORDS BROKEN AT THE FAIR: 3

According to Guinness World Records, Minefaire 2016, a gathering of *Minecraft* fans, was the biggest convention ever for a single video game. Held October 15–16, at the Greater Philadelphia Expo Center in Oaks, Pennsylvania, the event attracted 12,140 people. Game developer Markus Persson created *Minecraft* in 2009 and sold it to Microsoft in 2014 for $2.5 billion. Gamers can play alone or with other players online. The game involves breaking and placing blocks to build whatever gamers can imagine—from simple constructions to huge virtual worlds. Attendance was not the only element of Minefaire to gain world-record status. On October 15 the largest-ever *Minecraft* architecture lesson attracted 342 attendees, and American gamer Lestat Wade broke the record for building the tallest staircase in *Minecraft* in one minute.

OPPORTUNITY

rover on mars

LONGEST-SURVIVING

Since January 2004, the Opportunity rover has been exploring planet Mars. The 384-pound NASA rover left Earth on July 7, 2003, to travel 283 million miles to Mars. Its twin rover, Spirit, left in June. The rovers, equipped with cameras and scientific equipment, landed on opposite sides of Mars and collected data on the planet's surface. NASA expected the mission to last ninety days but decided to keep the rovers on the Red Planet to explore further. NASA lost contact with Spirit in 2011, but Opportunity continues to roam Mars.

LARGEST single machine

LARGE HADRON COLLIDER

The Large Hadron Collider (LHC) is a 16-mile, ring-shaped machine that sits 328 feet below ground on the French/Swiss border. In 2008, the European Organization for Nuclear Research (CERN) switched on the machine that thousands of scientists and engineers spent years building. They hope that the gigantic collider will explain many mysteries of the universe by examining its tiniest particles, called hadrons. The machine makes these particles travel almost at the speed of light and records what happens when they collide. The aim is to examine various scientific theories, including the idea that the universe originated in a massive cosmic explosion known as the Big Bang.

119

Fanny is a massive 26-foot-high, 51-foot-long, fire-breathing dragon. She is also the world's biggest walking robot. In 2012, a German company designed and built Fanny using both hydraulic and electronic parts. She is radio remote-controlled with nine controllers, while 238 sensors allow the robot to assess her environment. She does this while walking on her four legs or stretching wings that span 39 feet. Powered by a 140-horsepower diesel engine, Fanny weighs a hefty 24,250 pounds—as much as two elephants—and breathes real fire using 24 pounds of liquid gas.

BIGGEST
walking robot
FANNY

FANNY STATS:

09/27/2012

DATE OF FANNY'S LAUNCH: **September 27, 2012**

26′ 10″

FANNY'S HEIGHT: **26 feet, 10 inches**

51′ 6″

FANNY'S LENGTH: **51 feet, 6 inches**

12′

FANNY'S BODY WIDTH: **12 feet**

39′

FANNY'S WINGSPAN: **39 feet**

VERSIUS

WORLD'S SMALLEST surgical robot

British robot specialists Cambridge Medical Robotics developed the world's smallest surgical robot in 2017. Operated by a surgeon using a console guide with a 3-D screen, the robot is able to carry out keyhole surgery. The scientists modeled the robot, called Versius, on the human arm, giving it similar wrist joints to allow maximum flexibility. Keyhole surgery involves making very small cuts on the surface of a person's body, through which a surgeon can operate. The recovery time of the patient is usually quicker when operated on in this way.

FASTEST
remote-controlled car

BLACK KNIGHT

Built and driven by Anthony Lovering from the United Kingdom, and reaching speeds of more than 200 miles per hour, Black Knight is the world's fastest rocket-powered remote-controlled car. On May 4, 2016, Black Knight hit a speed of 210.11 mph at Snowdonia Aerospace LLP, in Llanbedr, U.K., setting a Guinness World Record that remains unbeaten. Lovering is cofounder of an organization called ROSSA, the Radio Operated Scale Speed Association, which holds events all over the world to find the fastest remote-controlled vehicles.

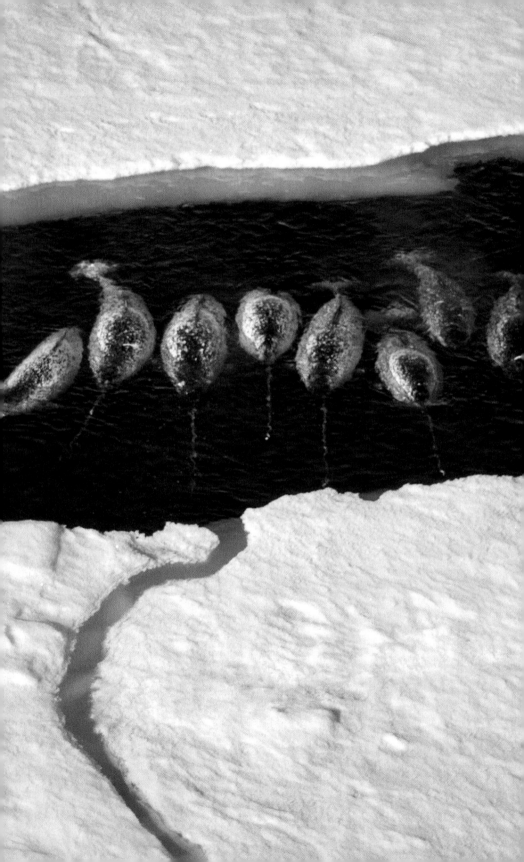

amazing
ANIMALS

WILD ANIMALS
TRENDING

GLOWING TURTLE
Rare turtle proves even rarer

In 2017 marine biologist David Gruber spotted a glowing sea turtle in the waters around the Solomon Islands. Although there are many species of fish known to glow, this characteristic has never been seen in a marine reptile before. The ability to reflect blue light as a different color—green, red, and orange—is called biofluorescence.

RARE SPECIES FACES EXTINCTION
Sudan the white rhino dies

On March 19, 2018, wildlife rangers at Ol Pejeta Conservancy in northern Kenya reported the death of forty-five-year-old Sudan, the world's last male northern white rhinoceros. His death marked a sad day for the natural world. Two females—also the last remaining of their species—live at the same conservancy. Now that they have no male rhino to mate with, the species cannot survive.

SUPERSIZED SHARK
Viral undersea video clip

With more than 10 million views on YouTube, video footage of a great white shark went viral in 2017. Posted by Mauricio Hoyos Padilla, the video, titled "Deep Blue," showed footage of a massive great white shark swimming off the coast of Mexico's Guadalupe Island. The shark was 20 feet long, and scientists think it could be the largest great white ever caught on camera.

NEW SPECIES DISCOVERED
Bhupathy's purple pig-nose frog

The discovery was made, in 2017, of a new species of purple frog. Puffed up, with shiny purple skin, a piglike snout, and a blue ring around its eyes, the creature was found by scientists in India's Western Ghats mountain range. The frog spends most of its life underground, coming out to mate when it rains.

SMALL FLY WITH A BIG NAME
Fly named for Schwarzenegger

In January 2018, scientist Brian Brown at the Natural History Museum of Los Angeles County named a fly for Arnold Schwarzenegger on account of its extraordinarily strong legs. Measuring just 0.395 mm and almost invisible to the naked eye, *Megapropodiphora arnoldi* is the smallest known fly in the world.

127

WORLD'S sleepiest animal
KOALA

Australia's koala sleeps for up to twenty hours a day, and still manages to look sleepy when awake. This is due to the koala's unbelievably monotonous diet. It feeds, mostly at night, on the aromatic leaves of eucalyptus trees. The leaves have little nutritional or calorific value, so the marsupial saves energy by snoozing. It jams its rear end into a fork in the branches of its favorite tree so it cannot fall out while snoozing.

WORLD'S
best glider

Flying squirrels are champion animal gliders. The Japanese giant flying squirrel has been scientifically recorded making flights of up to 164 feet from tree to tree. These creatures have been estimated to make 656-foot flights when flying downhill. The squirrel remains aloft using a special flap of skin on either side of its body, which stretches between wrist and ankle. Its fluffy tail acts as a stabilizer to keep it steady, and the squirrel changes direction by twisting its wrists and moving its limbs.

FLYING SQUIRREL

WORLD'S GLIDERS
Distance in feet

Flying squirrel 656

Flying fish 655

Colugo, or flying lemur 230

Draco flying lizard 197

Flying squid 164

WORLD'S
heaviest land
mammal

AFRICAN
ELEPHANT

The African bush elephant is the world's largest living land animal. The biggest known bush elephant stood 13.8 feet at the shoulder and had an estimated weight of 13.5 tons. It is also the animal with the largest outer ears. The outsized flappers help keep the animal cool on the open savanna. The Asian elephant has much smaller earflaps, because it lives in the forest and is not exposed to the same high temperatures.

WORLD'S
tiniest bat
KITTI'S HOG-NOSED BAT

This little critter, the Kitti's hog-nosed bat, is just 1.3 inches long, with a wingspan of 6.7 inches, and weighs 0.07–0.10 ounces. It's tied for first place as world's smallest mammal with Savi's pygmy shrew, which is longer at 2.1 inches but lighter at 0.04–0.06 ounces. The bat lives in west central Thailand and southeast Myanmar, and the shrew is found from the Mediterranean to Southeast Asia.

WORLD'S LARGEST
primate
GORILLA

The largest living primates are the eastern gorillas, and the biggest subspecies is the very rare mountain gorilla. The tallest known was an adult male silverback, named for the color of the fur on his back. He stood at 6.4 feet tall, but he was an exception—silverbacks generally grow no bigger than 5.9 feet tall. Gorillas have long arms: The record holder had an arm span measuring 8.9 feet, while adult male humans have an average arm span of just 5.9 feet.

132

MOST COLORFUL monkey in the world
MANDRILL

The male mandrill's face is as flamboyant as his rear end. The vivid colors of both are brightest at breeding time. The colors announce to his rivals that he is an alpha male and he has the right to breed with the females. His exceptionally long and fang-like canine teeth reinforce his dominance. As his colors fade, so does his success with the ladies. Even so, he is still the world's largest monkey, as well as the most colorful.

WORLD'S FASTEST
land animal
CHEETAH

The fastest reliably recorded running speed of any animal was that of a zoo-bred cheetah that reached an incredible 65 miles per hour on a flat surface. Another captive cheetah, this time at Cincinnati Zoo, clocked 61 miles per hour from a standing start in 2012.

More recently, wild cheetahs have been timed while actually hunting their prey in the bush in Botswana. Using GPS technology and special tracking collars, the scientists found that these cheetahs had a top speed of 58 miles per hour over rough terrain.

FASTEST LAND ANIMALS
Speed in miles per hour

Cheetah 65   **Ostrich 60**   **Pronghorn 55**   **Springbok 55**   **Lion 30**

WORLD'S FASTEST fish
BLACK MARLIN

Timing the world's fastest fish relies on how fast a hooked fish pulls the line from a fisherman's reel, so part of its escape is by swimming and part by leaping. Using this method, sailfish, marlin, and swordfish come out on top. The sailfish was credited with 68 miles per hour in the 1930s. A BBC film crew claimed 80 miles per hour for a black marlin in 2001. Then, in a Japanese computer simulation in 2008, scientists calculated that a swordfish could reach 81 miles per hour. But this has not yet been proven in real trials, so the black marlin stays on top for now.

WORLD'S BIGGEST
big cat

TIGER

There are only five big cats: tiger, lion, jaguar, leopard, and snow leopard. The biggest and heaviest is the Siberian, or Amur, tiger, which lives in the taiga (boreal forest) of eastern Siberia, where it hunts deer and wild boar. The largest reliably measured tigers have been about 11.8 feet long and weighed 705 pounds, but there have been claims for larger individuals, such as the male shot in the Sikhote-Alin Mountains in 1950. That tiger weighed 847 pounds.

land animal

HOWLER MONKEY

The howler monkeys of Latin America are deafening. Males have an especially large hyoid bone. This horseshoe-shaped bone in the neck creates a chamber that makes the monkey's deep guttural growls sound louder for longer.

It is said that their calls can be heard up to 3 miles away. Both males and females call, and they holler mainly in the morning. It is thought that these calls are often one troop telling neighboring troops where they are.

Giraffes living on the savannas of eastern and southern Africa are the world's tallest animals. The tallest known bull giraffe measured 19 feet from the ground to the top of his horns. He could have looked over the top of a London double-decker bus or peered into the upstairs window of a two-story house. Despite having considerably longer necks than we do, giraffes have the same number of neck vertebrae. They also have long legs with which they can either speedily escape from predators or kick them to keep them away.

GIRAFFE STATS

6
HEIGHT OF A CALF AT BIRTH: 6 feet

25
AVERAGE LIFE SPAN: 25 years

100
ADULT'S DAILY FOOD CONSUMPTION:
100 pounds of leaves and twigs

WORLD'S TALLEST

living animal

GIRAFFE

REACHING GREAT HEIGHTS

A giraffe's tongue can grow up to 21 inches in length. This helps the animal reach leaves on the topmost branches of a tree when it is looking for food.

WORLD'S LONGEST tooth
NARWHAL

The narwhal's "sword" is an enormously elongated spiral tooth, or tusk. It can grow to more than 8.2 feet long. Several functions have been suggested for the tusk, from an adornment to attract the opposite sex—like a peacock's tail—to a sensory organ that detects changes in the seawater, such as saltiness, which could help the narwhal find food. Observers have noted that the larger a male narwhal's tusk, the more attractive he is to females.

THE WORLD'S LARGEST
living animal
BLUE WHALE

Blue whales are truly colossal. The largest one accurately measured was 110 feet long, and the heaviest weighed 209 tons. They feed on tiny krill, which they filter from the sea. On land, the largest known animal was a Titanosaur—a huge dinosaur that lived in what is now Argentina 101 million years ago. A skeleton found in 2014 suggests the creature was 121 feet long and weighed 77 tons. It belongs to a young Titanosaur, so an adult may have been bigger than a blue whale.

WORLD'S BIGGEST fish
WHALE SHARK

Recognizable from its spotted skin and enormous size, the whale shark is the world's largest living fish. It grows to a maximum length of about 66 feet. Like the blue whale, this fish feeds on some of the smallest creatures: krill, marine larvae, small fish, and fish eggs. The whale shark is also a great traveler: One female was tracked swimming 4,800 miles from Mexico—where hundreds of whale sharks gather each summer to feed—to the middle of the South Atlantic Ocean, where it is thought she may have given birth.

THE SHARK MOST DANGEROUS
to people
GREAT WHITE SHARK

SHARK ATTACKS
Number of humans attacked

Great white 314

Tiger shark 111

Bull shark 100

Sand tiger shark 29

The great white shark is at the top of the list for the highest number of attacks on people. The largest reliably measured fish was 21 feet long, making it the largest predatory fish in the sea. Its jaws are lined with large, triangular, serrated teeth that can slice through flesh, sinew, and even bone. However, there were just eighty-eight reported nonprovoked attacks by sharks of any kind in 2017, and only five of those proved fatal. Humans are not this creature's top food of choice. People don't have enough fat on their bodies. Mature white sharks prefer blubber-rich seals, dolphins, and whales. It is likely that many of the attacks on people are probably cases of mistaken identity.

WORLD'S LARGEST
crustacean
JAPANESE SPIDER CRAB

The deepwater Japanese spider crab has the largest leg span of any known crab or lobster. It comes a close second to the American lobster (the world's heaviest crustacean) by weight, and its gangly limbs can be extraordinarily long. The first European to discover this species found two sets of claws, measuring 10 feet long, propped up against a fisherman's hut. The crab must have been about 22 feet from one claw tip to the other when its limbs were spread apart.

The reticulated python of Indonesia is the world's longest snake. One, called Fragrant Flower, counts among the longest pythons ever discovered. It was living in the wilds of Java until villagers captured it. A local government official confirmed it was 48.8 feet long and weighed 985 pounds. These creatures are constricting snakes: They squeeze the life out of their prey. In 1999, a 22.9-foot-long python swallowed a sun bear in Balikpapan, East Kalimantan.

WORLD'S
LONGEST
snake
PYTHON

WORLD'S
largest
lizard

KOMODO
DRAGON

There are dragons on Indonesia's Komodo Island, and they're dangerous. The Komodo dragon's jaws are lined with sixty replaceable, serrated, backward-pointing teeth. Its saliva is laced with deadly bacteria and venom that the dragon works into a wound, ensuring its prey will die quickly. Prey can be as big as a pig or deer, because this lizard is the world's largest. It can grow up to 10.3 feet long and weigh 366 pounds.

WORLD'S SMALLEST owl
NORTH AMERICAN ELF OWL

FIVE OF THE WORLD'S OWLS
Height in inches

North American elf owl 5   **Little owl 8.7**   **Barn owl 15**   **Snowy owl 28**   **Great gray owl 33**

The North American elf owl is one of three tiny owls vying for this title. It is about 5 inches long and weighs 1.5 ounces. This owl spends winter in Mexico and flies to nest in Arizona and New Mexico in spring. It often occupies cavities excavated by woodpeckers in saguaro cacti. Rivals for the title of smallest owl are Peru's long-whiskered owlet and Mexico's Tamaulipas pygmy owl, which are both a touch shorter but slightly heavier, making the elf owl the smallest of all.

WORLD'S
smelliest
bird
HOATZIN

The hoatzin eats leaves, flowers, and fruit, and ferments the food in its crop (a pouch in its esophagus). This habit leaves the bird with a foul odor, which has led people to nickname the hoatzin the "stinkbird." About the size of a pheasant, this bird lives in the Amazon and Orinoco river basins of South America. A hoatzin chick has sharp claws on its wings, like a pterodactyl. If threatened by a snake, the chick jumps from the nest into the water, then uses its wing claws to help it climb back up.

bird with the
LONGEST TAIL
RIBBON-TAILED ASTRAPIA

The ribbon-tailed astrapia has the longest feathers in relation to body size of any wild bird. The male, which has a beautiful, iridescent blue-green head, sports a pair of white ribbon-shaped tail feathers that are more than 3.3 feet long—three times the length of its 13-inch-long body. It is one of Papua New Guinea's birds of paradise and lives in the mountain forests of central New Guinea, where males sometimes have to untangle their tails from the foliage before they can fly.

BIRD WITH THE LONGEST wingspan

WANDERING ALBATROSS

Long, narrow wings, like those of a glider aircraft, are the mark of the wandering albatross. The longest authenticated measurement for wingspan was taken in 1965 from an old-timer, its pure-white plumage an indication of its age. Its wingspan was 11.9 feet. This seabird rarely flaps its wings, but uses the wind and updrafts from waves to soar effortlessly over the ocean.

BIRDS WITH LONG WINGSPANS
Wingspan in feet

Wandering albatross 11.9

Great white pelican 11.81

Andean condor 10.5

Marabou stork 10.5

Southern royal albatross 9.8

BIRD WITH THE STRONGEST
forehead

The helmeted hornbill is a real bruiser. It has a structure, known as a casque, sitting atop its chisel-like bill. Unlike other hornbills, which have hollow casques, the helmeted hornbill has an almost solid one. It is filled with "hornbill ivory," which is even more valuable than elephant ivory in southern Asia. The bill and casque weigh more than 10 percent of the bird's body weight. Males use their heads as battering rams, slamming casques together in fights over territory.

HELMETED HORNBILL

BIRD THAT BUILDS
largest nest
BALD EAGLE

THE WORLD'S LARGEST NESTS
Diameter in inches

Bald eagle 114

Golden eagle 55

White stork 57

With a wingspan over 6.6 feet, bald eagles need space to land and take off—so their nests can be gargantuan. Over the years, a nest built by a pair of bald eagles in St. Petersburg, Florida, has taken on epic proportions. Measuring 9.5 feet across and 20 feet deep, it is made of sticks, grass, and moss. At one stage it was thought to have weighed at least 2 tons, making it the largest nest ever constructed by a pair of birds. Although only one pair nests at any one time, these huge structures are often the work of several pairs of birds, each building on top of the work of their predecessors.

5.9 in

4.5 in

WORLD'S
largest bird egg
AFRICAN OSTRICH EGG

The ostrich lays the largest eggs of any living bird, yet they are the smallest eggs relative to the size of the mother's body. Each egg is some 5.9 inches long and weighs about 3.5–5 pounds, while the mother is about 6.2 feet tall and the male 1.6 feet taller, making the ostrich the world's largest living bird. The female lays about fifty eggs per year, and each egg contains as much yolk and albumen as twenty-four hens' eggs. It takes an hour to soft boil an ostrich egg!

CHILLY HOME
Emperor penguins live year-round
in Antarctica. Temperatures here are
freezing and can drop to −76°F.

EMPEROR
PENGUIN STATS

80

AVERAGE WEIGHT OF AN ADULT:
80 pounds

1,640

DEPTHS AN ADULT CAN SWIM TO:
1,640 feet

22

LENGTH OF TIME UNDERWATER:
Up to 22 minutes

FIVE OF THE WORLD'S
PENGUINS
Height in inches

Emperor 48   King 39   Gentoo 35   Macaroni 28   Galápagos 19

WORLD'S BIGGEST
penguin

EMPEROR PENGUIN

At 4 feet tall, the emperor penguin is the world's biggest living penguin. It has a most curious lifestyle, breeding during the long, dark Antarctic winter. The female lays a single egg and carefully passes it to the male. She heads out to sea to feed, while he remains with the egg balanced on his feet and tucked under a fold of blubber-rich skin. There he stands with all the other penguin dads, huddled together to keep warm in the blizzards and 100-mile-per-hour winds that scour the icy continent. Come spring, the egg hatches, the female returns, and mom and dad swap duties, taking turns to feed and care for their fluffy chick.

LARGEST-EVER
bee beard
JUAN CARLOS NOGUEZ ORTIZ

On August 30, 2017, Canadian Juan Carlos Noguez Ortiz made bee-beard history sitting calmly in Yonge-Dundas Square, Toronto, with thousands of bees on his face. As a crowd of onlookers gathered to watch, he stayed covered for 61 minutes, breaking the previous record of 53 minutes, 34 seconds. Employed by Dickey Bee Honey Farm in Cookstown, Ontario, Ortiz claimed to have practiced only twice before setting the new record, stating that he "wanted to show people that they don't have to be scared of the bees."

WORLD'S FASTEST

flying
insect
DESERT
LOCUST

Flying insects are difficult to clock, and many crazy speeds have been claimed. The fastest airspeed reliably timed was by fifteen desert locusts that managed an average of 21 miles per hour. Airspeed is the actual speed at which the insect flies. It is different from ground speed, which is often enhanced by favorable winds.

A black cutworm moth whizzed along at 70 miles per hour while riding the winds ahead of a cold front. The most shocking measurement, however, is that of a horsefly with an estimated airspeed of 90 miles per hour while chasing an air-gun pellet! The speed, understandably, has not been verified.

WORLD'S
DEADLIEST
animal
MOSQUITO

Female mosquitoes live on the blood of birds and mammals—humans included. However, the problem is not what they take, but what they leave behind. In a mosquito's saliva are organisms that cause the world's most deadly illnesses, including malaria, yellow fever, dengue fever, West Nile virus, and encephalitis. It is estimated that mosquitoes transmit diseases to a staggering 700 million people every year, of which 725,000 die. Mosquitoes are the deadliest family of insects on Earth.

WORLD'S HEAVIEST spider
GOLIATH BIRD-EATING TARANTULA

FOUR OF THE WORLD'S SPIDERS
Leg span in inches

**Giant huntsman
spider 12**

**Goliath bird-eating
tarantula 11**

**Brazilian wandering
spider 5.9**

**Golden silk
orb-weaver 5**

The size of a dinner plate, the female goliath bird-eating tarantula has a leg span of 11 inches and weighs up to 6.17 ounces. This is the world's heaviest spider and a real nightmare for an arachnophobe (someone with a fear of spiders). Its fangs can pierce a person's skin, but its venom is no worse than a bee sting. The hairs on its body are more of a hazard. When threatened, it rubs its abdomen with its hind legs and releases tiny hairs that cause severe irritation to the skin. Despite its name, this spider does not actually eat birds very often.

TRENDING#
PET ANIMALS

POPULAR PIG
Esther the Wonder Pig

Esther the Wonder Pig became an Internet sensation in 2017, attracting more than 1.3 million followers on Facebook. Originally thought by owners Steve Jenkins and Derek Walter to be a "micro" pig, Esther grew to a massive 650 pounds. Her amusing antics were so entertaining that when Jenkins and Walter started a Facebook page for her, she attracted a good deal of attention. Numerous fans sent her clothes to dress up in, which increased her popularity. The couple has since used Esther's popularity to raise money for an animal sanctuary in rural Ontario, Canada, and in 2017, Esther published her life story, *Esther the Wonder Pig*.

DACHSHUND GET-TOGETHER
World record broken twice

On March 25, 2018, the Cornwall Dachshund Walkers broke the world record for the most dachshunds in one place. The 601 dogs gathered at Perranporth Beach, Cornwall, England, breaking the previous record of 500. Two weeks later, on April 8, 2018, a mass dachshund walk at Manchester's Heaton Park attracted 1,239 dogs, doubling the previous record.

THE DODO
No. 1 digital media brand

Present on Facebook, YouTube, Instagram, Twitter, and Snapchat, The Dodo dominated the pet sphere in 2017. The brand's content is packed with entertaining and inspiring stories about animals, averaging 2.4 billion video views per month. Some videos gain millions of views—for example, the story of a Siberian Husky that adopted a kitten (6.3 million views) or the man who gave a drowning puppy CPR (5.8 million views).

CANINE CAREERS
LCC K-9 Comfort Dogs

The Lutheran Church Charities K-9 Comfort Dog Ministry was launched in August 2008. Its members are purebred golden retrievers—dogs known for their intelligence and loyalty. In recent years, the dogs have been deployed to help people deal with traumatic events, such as the mass shooting that killed fifty-eight people on October 1, 2017, in Las Vegas at the Route 91 Harvest festival. A team of twenty-two LCC K-9 Comfort Dogs were sent to Las Vegas to bring solace to the people most affected by the shooting—the first responders and victims' families.

SUPERSIZED CHICKEN GOES VIRAL
Brahma chicken freaks Twitter users

A video posted on Twitter in March 2017 went viral when people couldn't believe the size of the chicken it featured. The giant black-and-white feathered bird took the Twittersphere by storm. It turned out that the chicken was a member of a species known as the Brahma chicken, which can grow to weigh 18.25 pounds.

WORLD'S FLUFFIEST
rabbit
ANGORA RABBIT

In most people's opinion, the Angora rabbit is the world's fluffiest bunny. The breed originated in Turkey and is thought to be one of the world's oldest rabbit breeds as well. It became popular with the French court in the mid-eighteenth century. Today it is bred for its long, soft, wool, which is shorn every three to four months. One of the fluffiest bunnies is buff-colored Franchesca, owned by English Angora rabbit expert Dr. Betty Chu. In 2014, Franchesca's fur was measured at 14.37 inches, making a world record that is yet to be beaten.

Thumbelina is a dwarf miniature horse. At just 17.5 inches tall and weighing 60 pounds, she is officially the world's smallest horse. She is stout with unusually short limbs, a far cry from the long-legged Big Jake, the world's tallest horse: a Belgian gelding at 6.9 feet.

THE WORLD'S SMALLEST
horse
THUMBELINA

WORLD'S HAIRIEST dog
KOMONDOR

The world's hairiest dog breed is the komondor, or Hungarian sheepdog. It is a powerful dog that was bred originally to guard sheep. Its long, white, dreadlock-like "cords" enable it not only to blend in with the flock, but also protect itself from bad weather and bites from wolves. This is a large dog, standing over 27.5 inches at the shoulders. Its hairs are up to 10.6 inches long, giving it the heaviest coat of any dog.

dog breed
LABRADOR

The Labrador retriever holds the top spot as America's most popular breed of dog for a record-breaking 27th consecutive year. Its eager-to-please temperament makes it an ideal companion. The Labrador was originally bred as a gun dog that fetched game birds shot by hunters. Now, aside from being a family pet, it is a favored assistance dog that helps blind people, and a good detection dog used by law-enforcement agencies.

AMERICA'S MOST POPULAR DOGS
Rating
1 LABRADOR RETRIEVER
2 GERMAN SHEPHERD
3 GOLDEN RETRIEVER
4 FRENCH BULLDOG
5 BULLDOG
6 BEAGLE
7 POODLE
8 ROTTWEILER
9 YORKSHIRE TERRIER
10 POINTER

WORLD'S TALLEST living dog FREDDY

At 40.75 inches tall, a Great Dane called Freddy claimed the title world's tallest living dog in December 2016 and holds the record to this day. He lives in the United Kingdom with his owner, Claire Stoneman, and his sister Fleur. According to Claire, her two pets cost her around $1,400 a year in food alone, with Freddy eating 2.2 pounds of ground beef, 10.5 ounces of liver, and 9 ounces of steak a day. When Freddy stands on his hind legs, he towers over his owner at a height of 90 inches.

WORLD'S

Chihuahuas are the world's smallest dog breed—and the smallest of them all is Miracle Milly, a Chihuahua from Puerto Rico. She measures just 3.8 inches tall, no bigger than a sneaker. The shortest is Heaven Sent Brandy from Florida, just 6 inches from her nose to the tip of her tail. Chihuahuas originated in Mexico, and may have predated the Maya. They are probably descendants of the Techichi, an early companion dog of the Toltec civilization (900–1168 CE).

smallest dog

CHIHUAHUA

AMERICA'S MOST POPULAR

cat breed
EXOTIC SHORTHAIR

The exotic has done it again! It is America's most popular breed of 2017, the third year in a row, according to the Cat Fanciers' Association. Its thick, short coat, giving the cat a teddy bear look, is easier to manage than the long coat of the Persian, and its round, Garfield-like face is as appealing as the cartoon cat itself. A calm and friendly breed, the exotic shorthair is also recognized as an accomplished "mouser." The Ragdoll and British Shorthair, meanwhile, have pushed the Persian, once the top cat, into fourth place.

America's most popular cats
Rating

1 EXOTIC SHORTHAIR
2 RAGDOLL
3 BRITISH SHORTHAIR
4 PERSIAN
5 MAINE COON CAT
6 AMERICAN SHORTHAIR
7 SCOTTISH FOLD
8 SPHYNX
9 DEVON REX
10 ABYSSINIAN

cat

SPHYNX

The sphynx breed of cats is famous for its wrinkles and the lack of a normal coat, but it is not entirely hairless. Its skin is like the softest chamois leather, but it has a thin layer of down. It behaves more like a dog than a cat, greeting owners when they come home, and is friendly to strangers. The breed originated in Canada, where a black-and-white cat gave birth to a hairless kitten called Prune in 1966. Subsequent breeding gave rise to the sphynx.

7

incredible EARTH

INCREDIBLE EARTH
TRENDING#

EARTHQUAKE ZONE
Mexico hit twice in two weeks

On September 8, 2017, the most powerful earthquake to strike Mexico in one hundred years occurred. It measured 8.1 on the Richter scale. Its epicenter was 74 miles from Mexico's Pacific Ocean coastline and there were fewer than 100 deaths. Two weeks later an earthquake measuring 7.1 on the Richter scale occurred. This time, the epicenter was just 75 miles from Mexico City and the disaster resulted in 369 fatalities.

#ECLIPSE2017
The Great American Solar Eclipse

National Geographic won a Shorty Award for its live-streaming coverage of 2017's Great American Eclipse. With round-the-clock updates on what was happening, the science behind it, and stories relating to it, the company kept millions of people informed. Working across several platforms, *National Geographic* notched up 85 million impressions on Instagram and had a viewership of 3.5 million on its live-streaming channel on YouTube.

WORLD WATER MONTH
Raising awareness online

The beer giant Stella Artois joined *National Geographic* and Water.org to raise global awareness of the 663 million people around the world who have limited access to clean water. To give the campaign a boost, *National Geographic* made the most of its online presence, posting thirty photos on Instagram channels, adding ten posts on Facebook channels, and launching a Snapchat takeover.

LUNAR MARVEL
Year of the supermoon

On December 3, 2017, moon enthusiasts around the globe were treated to the moon shining bigger and brighter than usual. Not only was there a full moon that night, but it coincided with that time of the moon's orbit when it is closest to Earth. It meant that the moon appeared 7 percent larger and 16 percent brighter than usual. Another supermoon appeared a month later, on January 2, 2018.

FROZEN NIAGARA
Instagram fame

Niagara Falls in the state of New York and Canada was the most Instagrammed natural wonder of 2017. Around 3,160 tons of water flow over the edge of these giant waterfalls each second, and the site attracts 14 million visitors a year. Beautiful images of the falls were shared on the Internet when temperatures dropped as low as 14 degrees Fahrenheit toward the end of 2017 and into January 2018.

trees on earth OLDEST
BRISTLECONE PINE

An unnamed bristlecone pine in the White Mountains of California is the world's oldest continually standing tree. It is 5,065 years old, beating its bristlecone rivals the Methuselah (4,849 years old) and Prometheus (4,847 years old). Sweden is home to an even older tree, a Norway spruce (which are often used as Christmas trees) that took root about 9,550 years ago. However, this tree has not been standing continually, but is long-lived because it can clone itself. When the trunk dies, a new one grows up from the same rootstock, so in theory it could live forever.

WORLD'S TALLEST tree
CALIFORNIA REDWOOD

A coast redwood named Hyperion is the world's tallest known living tree. It is 379.1 feet tall, and could have grown taller if a woodpecker had not hammered its top. It's growing in a remote part of the Redwood National and State Parks in Northern California, but its exact location is kept a secret for fear that too many visitors would upset its ecosystem. It is thought to be 700 to 800 years old.

WORLD'S TALLEST TREES
Height in feet.

California redwood, California, USA 379.1

Mountain ash, Tasmania 327.4

Coast Douglas-fir, Oregon, USA 327.3

Sitka spruce, California, USA 317

Giant sequoia, California, USA 314

LARGEST AND HEAVIEST
fruit

The world's largest-ever fruit was a cultivated pumpkin grown by Swiss gardener Beni Meier, the first non-American giant pumpkin champion. His winning squash weighed an incredible 2,324 pounds, and Beni had to hire special transportation to take it for weighing in at the October 2014 European Championship Pumpkin Weigh-off, held in Germany. The seeds of nearly all giant pumpkins can trace their ancestry back to a species of squash that was cultivated by Canadian pumpkin breeder Howard Dill.

PUMPKIN

WORLD'S TOUGHEST leaf
AMAZON WATER LILY

The leaf of the giant Amazon water lily is up to 8.6 feet across. It has an upturned rim and a waxy, water-repellent upper surface. On the underside of the leaf is a strong, riblike structure that traps air between the ribs so the leaf floats easily. The ribs are also lined with sharp spines that protect them from aquatic plant eaters. The leaf is so large and so strong that it can support the weight of a child.

WORLD'S LARGEST
single flower
RAFFLESIA

The scent of dead and decaying meat is not the usual quality sought in a flower, but the flies and beetles on the islands of Borneo and Sumatra love it. *Rafflesia* is known locally as the corpse flower, and at 3.3 feet across, it is the world's largest. It has no obvious stems, leaves, or roots because it is a parasite, and the only time anyone sees it is when it flowers. A female flower has to be fairly close to a male flower for successful pollination, and that is rare, because groups of flowers tend to be either one gender or the other. With forests on the two islands dwindling, the future for *Rafflesia* looks bleak.

WORLD'S MOST DANGEROUS

mushroom
DEATH CAP

Don't eat the death cap—the warning is in the name. This fungus is responsible for the most deaths by mushroom poisoning and can be found all over the world, including the United States. The mushroom's toxins damage the liver and kidneys, and it is not possible to destroy the dangerous chemicals by cooking, freezing, or drying. The Roman emperor Claudius is thought to have died from death-cap poisoning in 54 CE. He liked to eat salads of Caesar mushrooms, an almost identical edible species, but was served the killer fungus instead.

EXTRAORDINARY LENGTHS
In order to establish the record-breaking depths of Krubera Cave, diver Gennady Samokhin had to descend as far down as 151 feet in an underwater channel.

The limestone-rich Western Caucasus in Georgia have some extraordinary cave systems. Among the caverns there is Krubera, the deepest-known cave on Earth. Explorers have descended 7,208 feet from the cave entrance, and they suspect there is even more to explore. The cave is named for the Russian geographer Alexander Kruber, but the Ukrainian cave explorers have dubbed it "Crows' Cave" due to the number of crows that nest around the entrance.

DEEPEST CAVE
on earth
KRUBERA

KRUBERA CAVE STATS

1963
YEAR OF DISCOVERY: 1963

7,208
DEPTH DISCOVERED TO DATE:
7,208 feet

2012
YEAR CURRENT DEPTH DISCOVERED
ESTABLISHED: 2012

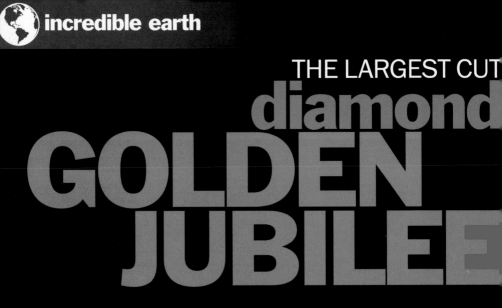

THE LARGEST CUT
diamond
GOLDEN JUBILEE

In 1985, South African miners chanced upon an enormous diamond. Jewel specialists worked for many years to hone it to perfection and fashioned a gem that was a staggering 545.67 carats, the largest cut diamond in the world. Pope John Paul II blessed the jewel, and the Thai royal family now owns it. For some time, the gem was known as Unnamed Brown, due to its color. Today it goes by the name of Golden Jubilee. If the diamond had been colorless, it would have been worth over $14 million—however, it is a yellow-brown color and worth "only" about $12 million.

GREATEST NUMBER
of geysers
YELLOWSTONE
NATIONAL
PARK

There are about 1,000 geysers that erupt worldwide, and 540 of them are in Yellowstone National Park, USA. That's the greatest concentration of geysers on Earth. The most famous is Old Faithful, which spews out a cloud of steam and hot water to a maximum height of 185 feet every 44 to 125 minutes. Yellowstone's spectacular water display is due to its closeness to molten rock from Earth's mantle that rises up to the surface. One day the park could face an eruption 1,000 times as powerful as that of Mt. St. Helens in 1980.

GEYSER FIELDS
Number of geysers

Yellowstone, Idaho, Montana, Wyoming, USA 540

Valley of Geysers, Kamchatka, Russia 139

El Tatio, Andes, Chile 84

Orakei Korako, New Zealand 33

Hveravellir, Iceland 16

29,029 feet

Mount Everest's snowy peak is an unbelievable 5.5 miles above sea level. This mega mountain is located in the Himalayas, on the border between Tibet and Nepal. The mountain acquired its official name from surveyor Sir George Everest, but local people know it as Chomolungma (Tibet) or Sagarmatha (Nepal). In 1953, Sir Edmund Hillary and Tenzing Norgay were the first to reach its summit. Now more than 650 people per year manage to make the spectacular climb.

MOUNT EVEREST is earth's TALLEST MOUNTAIN above sea level

WORLD'S TALLEST MOUNTAINS
Height above sea level in feet

Everest 29,029

K2 (Qogir) 28,251

Kanchenjunga 28,179

Lhotse 27,940

Makalu 27,838

WORLD'S GREATEST
barrier
REEF

Australia's Great Barrier Reef is the only living thing that's clearly visible from space. It stretches along the Queensland coast for 1,400 miles, making it the largest coral reef system in the world. The reef is home to an astounding number of animals: over 600 species of corals alone, 133 species of sharks and rays, and 30 species of whales and dolphins. In recent years, climate change has posed a huge threat to the world's coral reefs, with rising sea temperatures causing areas to die off. The northern half of the Great Barrier Reef suffered particularly in 2016, and scientists fear that more damage is yet to come.

WORLD'S LONGEST BARRIER REEFS
Length in miles

Great Barrier Reef, Australia 1,400

New Caledonia Barrier Reef, South Pacific 930

Mesoamerican Barrier Reef, Caribbean 620

Ningaloo Reef, Western Australia 162

WORLD'S LARGEST
hot desert
SAHARA DESERT

Sahara means simply "great desert," and great it is: It is the largest hot desert on the planet. It's almost the same size as the United States or China and dominates North Africa from the Atlantic Ocean in the west to the Red Sea in the east. It's extremely dry, with most of the Sahara receiving less than 0.1 inches of rain a year, and some places none at all for several years. It is stiflingly hot, up to 122°F, making it one of the hottest and driest regions in the world.

WORLD'S LARGEST HOT DESERTS
Size in square miles

Sahara Desert, North Africa
3.63 million

Arabian Desert, Western Asia
900,000

Great Victoria Desert, Australia 250,000

Kalahari Desert, Africa
220,000

Syrian Desert, Arabian peninsula
190,000

WORLD'S LARGEST lake
CASPIAN SEA

Russia, Kazakhstan, Turkmenistan, Iran, and Azerbaijan border the vast Caspian Sea, the largest inland body of water on Earth. Once part of an ancient sea, the lake became landlocked between five and ten million years ago, with occasional fills of salt water as sea levels fluctuated over time. Now it has a surface area of about 149,200 square miles and is home to one of the world's most valuable fish: the beluga sturgeon, the source of beluga caviar, which costs up to $2,250 per pound.

WORLD'S LARGEST LAKES
Area in square miles

Caspian Sea, Europe/ Asia 149,200

Lake Superior, North America 31,700

Lake Victoria, Africa 26,600

Lake Huron, North America 23,000

Lake Michigan, North America 22,300

WORLD'S LONGEST river
NILE RIVER

People who study rivers cannot agree on the Nile's source—nobody knows where it actually starts. Some say the most likely source is the Kagera River in Burundi, which is the farthest headstream (a stream that is the source of a river) to flow into Lake Victoria. From the lake, the Nile proper heads north across eastern Africa for 4,132 miles to the Mediterranean. Its water is crucial to people living along its banks. They use it to irrigate precious crops, generate electricity and, in the lower

WORLD'S LONGEST RIVERS
Length in miles

Yellow River, China 3,395

Mississippi–Missouri river system, USA 3,710

Yangtze River, China 3,915

Amazon River, South America 4,000

Nile River, Africa 4,132

WORLD'S TALLEST
surf waves

Many of the world's tallest waves occur at Nazaré, Portugal. In November 2017, this is where Brazilian surfer Rodrigo Koxa rode an 80-foot-high monster wave to seize the world record. The previous record holder, veteran surfer Garrett McNamara from Hawaii, had surfed a 78-foot-tall wave at the same spot in 2011. Nazaré's tallest wave is estimated to have been at least 100 feet tall, but the measurement was not confirmed.

NAZARÉ,
PORTUGAL

WORLD'S TALLEST WAVES
Height in feet (year)

Nazaré, Portugal 100 (2013)

Caledonia Star, South Atlantic 98.43 (2001)

Lituya Bay, Alaska 98 (1958)

Nazaré, Portugal 78 (2011)

Draupner Oil Platform, Norway 60.7 (1995)

WEATHER
TRENDING#↑

MOST GOOGLED TOPIC OF 2017
Hurricane Irma

Hurricane Irma, a Category 5 storm that hit the Caribbean and the American South in September 2017, was the most Googled topic of the year—not just in the United States, but across the globe. The storm lasted from August 31 to September 11, causing damage in eleven states across an east–west distance of 650 miles. The damage in some areas was devastating and included 95 percent of all buildings on the island of Barbuda in the Caribbean. Around 5.6 million people left their homes before Irma made landfall, flooding several U.S. cities and leaving them without electricity.

GLOBAL WARMING
Hottest year ever

Weather centers around the globe recorded the year 2017 as one of the hottest on record. While 2016 is officially the hottest year, the temperature rise was boosted by El Niño. The difference with 2017 is that it was the warmest without the influence of El Niño. Either way, higher temperatures form part of a trend that has been on the rise for several decades, with nine of the ten warmest years on record occurring since the year 2005.

SNOWMAN EXTRAVAGANZA
Record snowfall in Japan

When Japan was hit with the heaviest snowfall in four years in January 2018, people took to the streets to build an impressive range of snowmen. Many of them were inspired by characters in movies and video games, including the Minions from the hugely popular Despicable Me franchise. Other treats included pandas, Godzilla, and the national icon, Hello Kitty.

ORANGE SNOW
Sahara sand in Europe

Winds blowing across Europe in October 2017 had a curious effect on the weather, causing skies above England to glow orange. A similar phenomenon was recorded at the end of March 2018, when orange snow fell on the mountain slopes of Sochi in Russia, host city of the 2014 Winter Olympics. The strange phenomenon was caused by sand from North Africa's Sahara desert blowing across Eastern Europe and the dust mixing with the air and the snow.

WHITE SAHARA
Snow in Africa

Freak snow events dominated the news last year, but none can be weirder than snow falling in the Sahara desert. This has happened just three times in the last forty years. As much as 15 inches of snow fell in January 2018. Before that, snow settled for a day in December 2016. The third event—a snowstorm that lasted just half an hour—occurred way back in 1979.

COLDEST INHABITED PLACE
on earth
OYMYAKON

Extremely low air temperatures of −96.2°F in 1924 and −90°F in 1933 were recorded in the village of Oymyakon in eastern Russia, the lowest temperatures ever recorded in a permanently inhabited area. Only the Antarctic gets colder than this.

The five hundred people living in Oymyakon regularly experience temperatures below zero from September to May, with the December/January/February average falling well below −58°F. The town sits in a valley surrounded by snowy mountains.

COLDEST PLACES ON EARTH

Coldest temperature recorded on Earth: Vostok Station, Antarctica −128.6°F

Coldest inhabited place on Earth: Oymyakon, eastern Russia −96.2°F

Coldest annual mean temperature: Resolute, Canada 3.7°F

WORLD'S LARGEST ice sculpture
ICE HOTEL

OTHER ICE HOTELS
SnowCastle of Kemi, Finland
Hôtel de Glace, Quebec City, Canada
Bjorli Ice Lodge, Norway
Hotel of Ice at Bâlea Lac, Romania
Ice Village, Shimukappu, Japan

Want to sleep on a bed made of ice in subzero temperatures? That is the prospect for guests at the world's largest ice sculpture—the original Icehotel and art exhibition in Jukkasjärvi, 125 miles north of the Arctic Circle in Sweden. Here, the walls, floors, and ceilings of the sixty-five rooms are made of ice from the local Torne River and snow from the surrounding land. The beds, chairs, and tables—and even the bar and the drinks glasses standing on it—are made of ice. A neighboring ice church hosts one hundred weddings each winter. The hotel is open from December to April, after which it melts back into the wild.

MOST DEVASTATING
wildfire of 2017
THOMAS FIRE

The last few months of 2017 bore witness to a series of fires that laid to waste vast areas of California. The largest was the Thomas Fire, which started in the foothills above Thomas Aquinas College in Santa Paula on December 4, and burned for longer than one month. Fueled by fierce Santa Ana winds, the fire destroyed some 281,900 acres of land in total, much of it dry from lack of rainfall in the preceding months. Records show that seven of the state's largest fires have occurred since the year 2000.

DEADLY MUDSLIDES
It is thought that the Thomas Fire contributed to the deadly mudslides that hit Montecito, California, on January 9, 2018. After the land was left barren of the vegetation that would normally absorb rain, it gave way following flash flooding in the area, destroying fifty-nine homes and killing at least twenty people.

THOMAS FIRE STATS

2,800
The number of firefighters involved: 2,800

177
The cost of fighting the fire, in millions of dollars: $177

1,063
The number of structures destroyed by the fire: 1,063

10
The cost of the damage caused, in billions of dollars: $10

MOST INTENSE
storm to hit land
HAIYAN

Typhoon Haiyan is one of the most powerful storms ever recorded, and was the strongest-ever tropical storm to hit land. On November 8, 2013, it struck the Philippines, where it was known as Super Typhoon Yolanda.

Wind speeds reached 195 miles per hour, and vast areas of the islands were damaged or destroyed. Around eleven million people were affected: Many were made homeless, and at least 6,300 people were killed.

AMERICA'S MOST
costly tornado
THE JOPLIN TORNADO

On May 22, 2011, a multiple-vortex tornado about one mile wide swept through Joplin, Missouri, killing 161 people and injuring more than one thousand others. It was the deadliest tornado in the United States since the 1947 Glazier-Higgins-Woodward tornadoes in which 181 people lost their lives. With $2.8 billion's worth of damage, the Joplin tornado was by far the costliest tornado in U.S. history. It was registered as an EF5 category tornado—the most intense kind—with winds in excess of 200 miles per hour. It ripped houses off their foundations and lifted cars and trucks into the air.

HIGHEST TSUNAMI in the United States
LITUYA BAY

On July 9, 1958, a severe 7.8 magnitude earthquake triggered a huge rockslide into the narrow inlet of Lituya Bay, Alaska. The sudden displacement of water caused a mega tsunami, with a crest estimated to be 98 feet tall. The giant wave traveled across the bay and destroyed vegetation up to 1,722 feet above sea level. Five people died, and nearby settlements, docks, and boats were damaged. It was the highest tsunami to be recorded in the United States in modern times.

MOST DESTRUCTIVE
storm surge in the
United States

When Hurricane Katrina slammed into the Louisiana coast in 2005, a storm surge drove the sea almost 12.5 miles inland. New Orleans's hurricane surge protection was breached in fifty-three places, levees failed, boats and barges rammed buildings, and the city and countless neighboring communities were severely flooded. About 80 percent of New Orleans was underwater, close to 1,833 people lost their lives, and an area almost the size of the United Kingdom was devastated. The damage cost an estimated $108 billion. The U.S. Homeland Security secretary described the aftermath of the hurricane as "probably the worst catastrophe, or set of catastrophes" in the country's history.

HURRICANE KATRINA

MOST POWERFUL HURRICANES IN THE UNITED STATES
Wind speed in miles per hour

Labor Day Hurricane (1935) 185

Hurricane Andrew (1992) 177

Hurricane Katrina (2005) 175

Galveston Hurricane (1900) 145

HOTTEST YEAR on record 2016

Data gathered by NASA's Goddard Institute for Space Studies shows that 2016 was the warmest year since records began in 1880. Global average temperatures were 1.78°F warmer than they were in the mid-twentieth century, and it was the third year in a row that global temperature records were broken, continuing a long-term warming trend. Most scientists agree that this temperature increase is caused by a rise in the greenhouse gas carbon dioxide and other human-made emissions in the atmosphere.

MOST SNOWFALL
in the United States

The greatest depth of snow on record in the United States occurred at Tamarack, near the Bear Valley ski resort in California, on March 11, 1911. The snow reached an incredible 37.8 feet deep. Tamarack also holds the record for the most snowfall in a single month, with 32.5 feet in January 1911. Mount Shasta, California, had the most snowfall in a single storm with 15.75 feet falling from February 13–19, 1959. The most snow in twenty-four hours was a snowfall of 6.3 feet at Silver Lake, Colorado, on April 14–15, 1921.

CALIFORNIA AND COLORADO

WORLD'S LARGEST
hailstone
VIVIAN, SOUTH DAKOTA

In August 2010, the town of Vivian, South Dakota, was bombarded by some of the biggest hailstones ever to have fallen out of the sky. They went straight through roofs of houses, smashed car windshields, and stripped vegetation. Among them was a world record breaker, a hailstone the size of a volleyball. It was 8 inches in diameter and weighed 2.2 pounds.

THE HUMAN
lightning conductor

Roy Sullivan was a U.S. park ranger in Shenandoah National Park, Virginia. While going about his duties he was struck by lightning no fewer than seven times. He claimed he was also hit by lightning as a child, making a total of eight lightning strikes. It came to the point that whenever a faraway thunderstorm was heard approaching, his coworkers deliberately distanced themselves from him—just in case!

ROY SULLIVAN

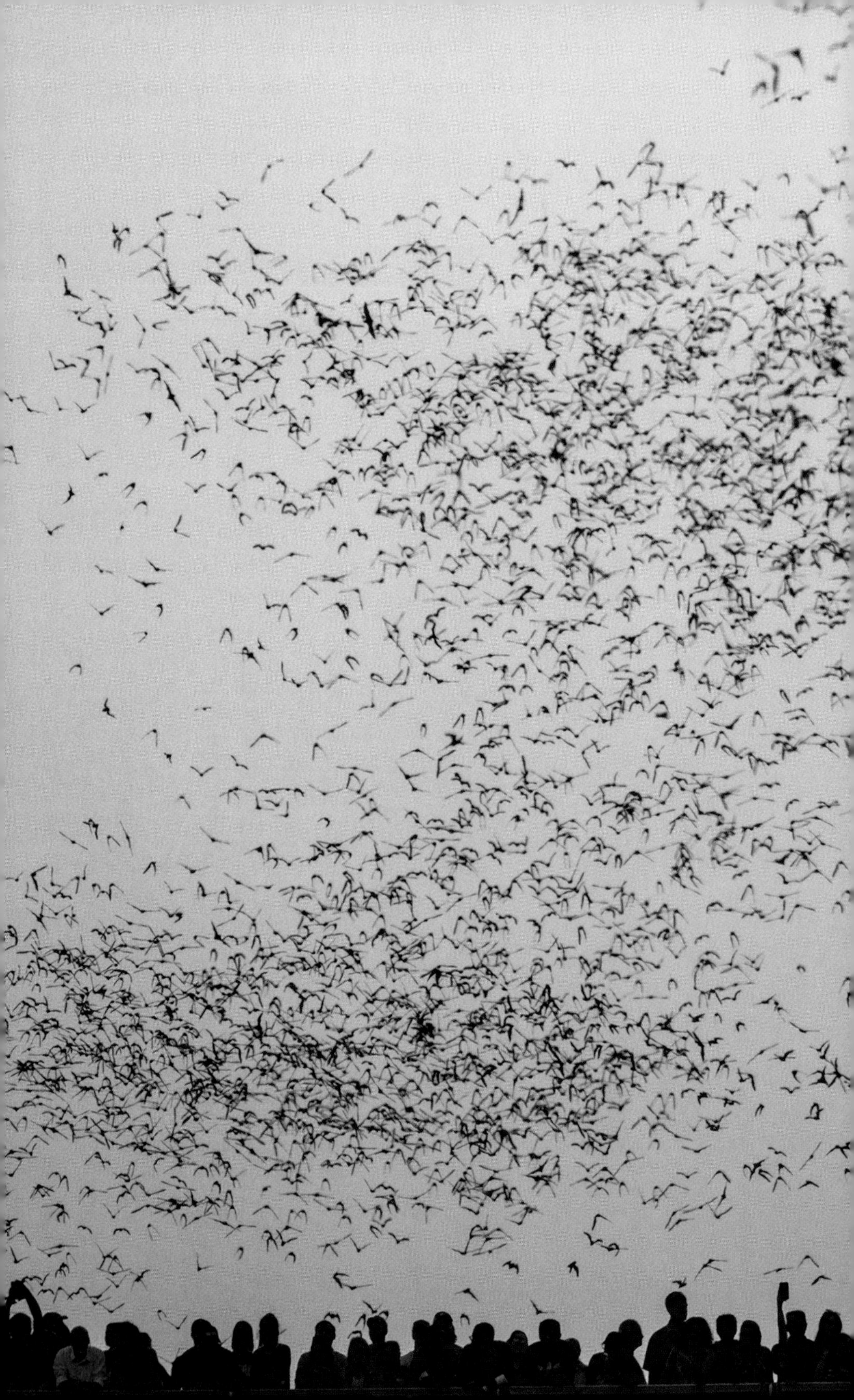

state
STATS

STATE STATS
TRENDING#

WE LOVE AMERICA
Instagram's most popular country

The United States scored seven out of ten in the world's most Instagrammed locations of 2017. Disneyland took the top spot with its original theme park in Anaheim, and came in sixth with Magic Kingdom, Orlando, and ninth with Disney California Adventure Park. New York had three winning locations: Times Square (second), Central Park (third), and the Brooklyn Bridge (eighth). The three non-American spots went to the Eiffel Tower and the Louvre, Paris, and Tokyo Disneyland.

DRESSED TO THE NINES
Llamas add drama to U.S. weddings

A new fad took off in 2017: renting llamas to make your wedding day truly unique. Couples in Portland, Oregon, and Vancouver, Washington, rented professional party llamas from Mtn Peaks Therapy Llamas & Alpacas in Vancouver. For fees starting at $200 per event, Rojo, Smokey, Diego, and Jean-Pierre arrived beautifully groomed and dressed in their festive finery, complete with bridal veils, top hats, and floral garlands around their necks.

ADD TO CART
U.S. online shopping trends

According to financial services company TD Securities, online shopping accounted for one-fifth of core purchases made in the U.S. in 2017. Attracted by the ease of use, ability to compare prices, and free shipping, customers are increasingly turning to the Internet for goods. By far the biggest e-commerce destination is Amazon, where 65 percent of Americans say they shop regularly—a figure that rose to 76 percent during the holiday season.

APRIL THE GIRAFFE
Millions track April's pregnancy

On April 15, 2017, 1.2 million people tuned in to the Animal Adventure Park Giraffe Cam in Harpursville, New York, to watch April the giraffe give birth to her son, Tajiri. Interest in April's story began in January, when the park posted an update on her pregnancy on Facebook. More and more people checked on the giraffe's progress over the next few weeks, so the park set up a live webcam via YouTube on February 10. A website followed on March 1.

AVATAR SENSATION
Disney's mega-attraction

On May 27, 2017, thrill seekers witnessed the opening of the largest attraction ever to be created at Disney's Animal Kingdom theme park. Inspired by the 2009 movie *Avatar*, the land is called Pandora—The World of Avatar. Filled with lush vegetation, Pandora has two rides: the Na'vi River Journey boat ride and Flight of Passage, which simulates a trip in the air, as if riding a banshee.

STATE WITH THE OLDEST

Mardi Gras celebration

ALABAMA

French settlers held the first American Mardi Gras in Mobile, Alabama, in 1703. Yearly celebrations continued until the Civil War and began again in 1866. Today 800,000 people gather in the city during the vibrant two-week festival. Dozens of parades with colorful floats and marching bands wind through the streets each day. Partygoers attend masked balls and other lively events sponsored by the city's social societies. On Mardi Gras, which means "Fat Tuesday" in French, six parades continue the party until the stroke of midnight, which marks the end of the year's festivities and the beginning of Lent.

STATE WITH THE MOST

pilots per capita

ALASKA

Alaska is the only state in the United States in which more than 1 percent of citizens have a pilot's license—no surprise, considering Alaska has many islands, and is the largest and most sparsely populated state. If you think this means the state has a surplus of skilled aviators, think again: Despite having six times the national average of pilots per capita, newspapers reported in 2016 that a pilot shortage in Alaska led the state to consider turning to drone technology. Many of its pilots and mechanics leave the state for high-flying careers in the lower forty-eight states.

MOST PILOTS PER CAPITA
Number of pilots per 100 people

Alaska 1.313

Montana 0.407

Colorado 0.393

North Dakota 0.383

Wyoming 0.363

STATE WITH THE BEST-PRESERVED
meteor crater
ARIZONA

Fifty thousand years ago, a meteor traveling at 26,000 miles per hour struck the Earth near present-day Winslow, Arizona, to create a mile-wide, 550-foot-deep crater. Today, Meteor Crater is a popular tourist destination, and is overseen by stewards who work to educate visitors about its formation. There is even an animated movie showing how it happened. The crater is sometimes known as the Barringer Crater, in recognition of mining engineer Daniel Moreau Barringer, who was the one to propose that it had been made by a meteorite. Previously, geologists had believed that the crater was a natural landform created over time.

ONLY STATE WHERE
diamonds are mined
ARKANSAS

Crater of Diamonds, near Murfreesboro, Arkansas, is the only active commercial diamond mine in the United States. Farmer and former owner John Wesley Huddleston first discovered diamonds there in August 1906, and a diamond rush overwhelmed the area after he sold the property to a mining company. For a time, there were two competing mines in this area, but in 1969, General Earth Minerals bought both mines to run them as private tourist attractions. Since 1972, the land has been owned by the state of Arkansas, which designated the area as Crater of Diamonds State Park. Visitors can pay a fee to search through plowed fields in the hope of discovering a gem for themselves.

MOST DEVOTED
theme-park fan
CALIFORNIA

On June 22, 2017, forty-four-year-old Jeff Reitz completed two thousand consecutive daily visits to the Disneyland and California Adventure Park in Anaheim, California. After finding himself unemployed, the Air Force veteran bought an annual pass to the theme park in a bid to cheer himself up. That was on January 1, 2012, and Jeff has visited the park every single day since then. These days, having found work, Jeff visits mostly in the evenings. When asked why he keeps coming back, he says it's all about enjoying the magic of the park. His favorite ride is the Matterhorn, a mountain-themed roller coaster on which passengers ride the rails in bobsleds.

STATE WITH THE LARGEST
elk population
COLORADO

Colorado is currently home to around 280,000 elk, making it the state with the largest elk population. Elk live on both public and private land across the state, from the mountainous regions to lower terrain. Popular targets for hunting, these creatures are regulated by both the Colorado Parks and Wildlife department and the National Park Service. Many elk live within the boundaries of Colorado's Rocky Mountain National Park. Elk are among the largest members of the deer family, and the males—called bulls—are distinguishable by their majestic antlers.

ONLY STATE TO MANUFACTURE PEZ candy CONNECTICUT

The PEZ factory in Orange, Connecticut, is the only place in the United States to make the world-famous candy. In 1927, an Austrian named Eduard Haas III invented PEZ as a breath mint. The letters come from the German word for peppermint, *Pfefferminz* (PfeffErminZ). The candy came to the United States in 1952, and the company opened its U.S. factory in 1975. Today, Americans consume an incredible three billion PEZ candies per year. The Visitor Center in Orange displays the largest collection of PEZ memorabilia on public display in the world, including the world's largest dispenser and a PEZ motorcycle.

STATE WITH THE MOST
horseshoe crabs
DELAWARE

Delaware Bay has the largest American horseshoe crab (*Limulus polyphemus*) population in the world. These creatures can be seen in large numbers on the bay's beaches in the spring. They appear during high tides on new and full moons, when they come onto land to spawn (deposit eggs). Horseshoe crabs—which are not actually related to other species of crab—have changed very little in the past 250 million years, and have therefore been called "living fossils." It is impossible to know the exact number of horseshoe crabs in the region, so every spring, volunteers at some of the state's beaches conduct counts to track spawning activity. In 2016, the Delaware Center for the Inland Bays reported a count of 15,418 horseshoe crabs across five beaches.

STATE WITH THE MOST-
visited amusement park
FLORIDA

Walt Disney World, in Lake Buena Vista, Florida, is home to several parks, including Magic Kingdom, the most- visited amusement park in the United States. Disney parks dominate the most-visited list, taking the top five spots. Magic Kingdom sees just over twenty million visitors from around the world who travel each year to ride the attractions, watch parades, and meet their favorite Disney characters. Divided into six themed areas, arguably the most iconic part of the park is Cinderella's Castle, which is illuminated each night by an impressive fireworks display and light-projection show.

MOST VISITED AMUSEMENT PARKS
Number of visitors per year in millions

Magic Kingdom, Walt Disney World, Florida 20.5

Disneyland, California 17.9

Epcot, Florida 11.8

Disney's Animal Kingdom, Florida 10.9

Disney's Hollywood Studios, Florida 10.8

STATE WITH THE LARGEST Sports Hall of Fame GEORGIA

At 43,000 square feet, Georgia's Sports Hall of Fame honors the state's greatest sports stars and coaches. The museum includes 14,000 square feet of exhibition space and a 205-seat theater. It owns more than 3,000 artifacts and memorabilia from Georgia's professional, college, and amateur athletes. At least 1,000 of these artifacts are on display at any time. The Hall of Fame corridor features over 300 inductees, such as golf legend Bobby Jones, baseball hero Jackie Robinson, and Olympic track medalist Wyomia Tyus.

ONLY STATE WITH

a royal palace

HAWAII

Iolani Palace, in downtown Honolulu, is the only official royal residence in the United States. The palace was built from 1879–1882 by King Kalakaua, inspired by the styles of the grand castles of Europe. The monarchs did not live there for long, however: In 1893, the kingdom of Hawaii was overthrown by U.S. forces.

Kalakaua's sister, Queen Liliuokalani, was even held prisoner in the palace in 1895 following a plot to put her back on the throne. Iolani Palace was used as a government building until it became a National Historic Landmark in 1962. Restored to its nineteenth-century condition, it is now open to the public as a museum.

FIRST STATE WITH a blue football field

Boise State's Albertsons Stadium, originally dubbed the "Smurf Turf" and now nicknamed "The Blue," was the first blue football field in the United States. In 1986, when the time came to upgrade the old turf, athletics director Gene Bleymaier realized that they would be spending a lot of money on the new field, yet most spectators wouldn't notice the difference. So, he asked AstroTurf to create the new field in the school's colors. Since the field's creation, students at the school have consistently voted for blue turf each time the field has been upgraded. Today, five more teams have opted for a colored playing field, including Eastern Washington, whose red field is dubbed "The Inferno," and Central Arkansas, where the teams play on purple and gray stripes.

IDAHO

STATE WITH THE OLDEST
free public zoo

Lincoln Park Zoo, in Chicago, Illinois, remains the oldest free public zoo in the United States. Founded in 1868—nine years after the Philadelphia Zoo, the country's oldest zoo overall—Lincoln Park Zoo does not charge admission fees. More than two-thirds of the money for the zoo's operating budget comes from food, retail, parking, and fund-raising events. Nonetheless, the zoo continues to grow. In November 2016, it opened a new exhibit—the Walter Family Arctic Tundra—to house its newest addition: a seven-year-old male polar bear named Siku.

Kovler
LION HOUSE

ILLINOIS

THE FIRST
professional baseball game

INDIANA

On May 4, 1871, the first National Association professional baseball game took place on Hamilton Field at Fort Wayne, Indiana. The home team, the Kekiongas, took on Forest City of Cleveland, beating them 2–0 against the odds. The Kekiongas were a little-known team at the time. In fact, this first game had been scheduled to take place between better-known Washington Olympic Club and the Cincinnati Red Stockings in Washington, DC, on May 3. Heavy rain forced a cancelation, however, and so history was made at Fort Wayne the following day.

STATE WITH THE SHORTEST STEEPEST railroad
IOWA

At only 296 feet long, Fenelon Place Elevator in Dubuque, Iowa, is the shortest railroad in the United States, and its elevation of 189 feet also makes it the steepest. The original railway was built in 1882 by businessman and former mayor J. K. Graves, who lived at the top of the Mississippi River bluff and wanted a quicker commute down into the town below. Today's railway, modernized in 1977, is open to the public. It costs $1.50 for an adult one-way trip, and consists of two quaint house-shaped cars traveling in opposite directions on parallel tracks.

STATE WITH THE MOST
rock concretions

Rock City, in Minneapolis, Kansas, boasts two hundred concretions of Dakota sandstone across a 5-acre park. They are the largest concretions in one place anywhere in the world. These concretions are huge spheres of rock, some of which measure up to 27 feet in diameter. They were created underground millions of years ago, when minerals deposited by water gradually formed hard, strong shells around small bits of matter in the sandstone. Over time, as the surrounding sandstone wore down, the concretions survived. Today, Rock City is a registered National Natural Landmark, and visitors can explore the park and climb the concretions for a $3.00 fee.

KANSAS

KENTUCKY

STATE WITH THE BIGGEST
fireworks display

The Kentucky Derby is the longest-running sporting event in the United States and proudly claims to be the "most exciting two minutes in sport." It's also accompanied by the biggest fireworks display held annually in the United States—"Thunder Over Louisville"—which kicks off the racing festivities. Zambelli Fireworks, which creates the display, says that the show requires nearly 60 tons of fireworks shells and a massive 700 miles of wire cable to sync the fireworks to music. The theme for the 2017 display was "Thunder: Local and Original."

STATE WITH THE MOST
crawfish
LOUISIANA

The majority of the crawfish consumed in the United States are caught in the state of Louisiana. While these critters may look like tiny lobsters, crawfish are actually freshwater shellfish, and are abundant in the mud of the state's bayous— sometimes they are called "mudbugs." Before white settlers arrived in Louisiana, crawfish were a favorite food of the native tribes, who caught them using reeds baited with venison. Today, crawfish are both commercially farmed and caught in their natural habitat. The industry yields between 120 and 150 million pounds of crawfish a year, and the crustaceans are an integral part of the state's culture, with backyard crawfish boils remaining a popular local tradition.

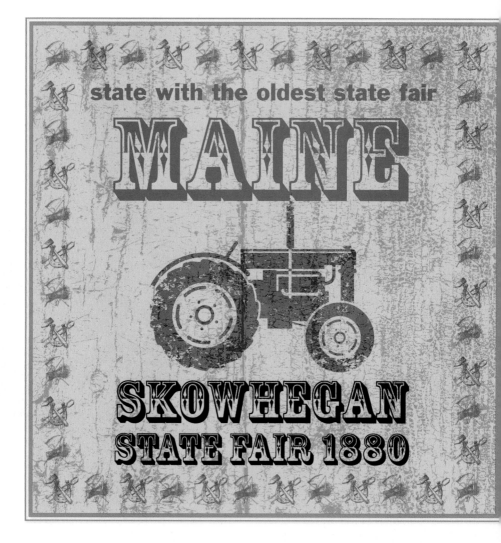

state with the oldest state fair

MAINE

SKOWHEGAN STATE FAIR 1880

In January 1819, the Somerset Central Agricultural Society sponsored the first-ever Skowhegan State Fair. In the 1800s, state fairs were important places for farmers to gather and learn about new agricultural methods and equipment. After Maine became a state in 1820, the fair continued to grow in size and popularity, gaining its official name in 1842. Today, the Skowhegan State Fair welcomes more than 7,000 exhibitors and 100,000 visitors. Enthusiasts can watch events that include livestock competitions, tractor pulling, a demolition derby, and much more during the ten-day show.

STATE WITH THE OLDEST
capitol building
MARYLAND

The Maryland State House in Annapolis is both the oldest capitol building in continuous legislative use and the only state house once to have been used as the national capitol. The Continental Congress met there from 1783–1784, and it was where George Washington formally resigned as commander in chief of the army following the American Revolution. The current building is the third to be erected on that site, and was actually incomplete when the Continental Congress met there in 1783, despite the cornerstone being laid in 1772. The interior of the building was finished in 1797, but not without tragedy—plasterer Thomas Dance fell to his death while working on the dome in 1793.

OLDEST CAPITOL BUILDINGS IN 2018
Age of building (year work was started)

Maryland 246 years (1772)

Virginia 233 years (1785)

New Jersey 226 years (1792)

Massachusetts 223 years (1795)

New Hampshire 202 years (1816)

STATE WITH THE OLDEST
Thanksgiving celebration

The first Thanksgiving celebration took place in 1621, in Plymouth, Massachusetts, when the Pilgrims held a feast to celebrate the harvest. They shared their meal with the native Wampanoag people from a nearby village. While the celebration became widespread in the Northeast in the late seventeenth century,

Thanksgiving was not celebrated nationally until 1863, when magazine editor Sarah Josepha Hale's writings convinced President Abraham Lincoln to make it a national holiday. Today, Plymouth, Massachusetts, holds a weekend-long celebration honoring its history: the America's Hometown Thanksgiving Celebration.

MOST MAGICAL state MICHIGAN

Colon, Michigan, is known as the magic capital of the world. The small town is home to Abbott Magic Company—one of the biggest manufacturers of magic supplies in the United States—as well as an annual magic festival, magicians' walk of fame, and Colon Lakeside Cemetery, in which twenty-eight magicians are buried. The Abbott plant boasts 50,000 square feet dedicated to creating new tricks— from simple silk scarves to custom illusions. It is the only building in the world expressly built for the purpose of making magic.

STATE WITH THE LARGEST
indoor amusement park

The biggest shopping mall in the United States is the Mall of America in Bloomington, Minnesota. The mall is home to Nickelodeon Universe, a 7-acre amusement park that features more than twenty rides. Avatar Airbender, Fairly Odd Coaster, and Shredder's Mutant Masher are among the favorites. Visitors can meet some of Nickelodeon's best-loved characters, such as SpongeBob SquarePants and Dora the Explorer. But that's not all: The park also offers an arcade, a zip line and ropes course, and an eighteen-hole miniature golf course.

MINNESOTA

MISSISSIPPI

only state to hold the International Ballet Competition

Every four years, Jackson, Mississippi, hosts the USA International Ballet Competition, a two-week Olympic-style event that awards gold, silver, and bronze medals. The competition began in 1964 in Varna, Bulgaria, and rotated among the cities of Varna; Moscow, Russia; and Tokyo, Japan. In June 1979, the competition came to the United States for the first time, and, in 1982, Congress passed a Joint Resolution designating Jackson as the official home of the competition. In addition to medals, dancers vie for cash prizes and the chance to join established ballet companies.

America's first ice-cream cone

MISSOURI

It is said that America's first ice-cream cone was introduced through chance inspiration at the St. Louis World's Fair in 1904. According to the most popular story, a Syrian salesman called Ernest Hamwi saw that an ice-cream vendor had plenty of ice cream but not enough cups and spoons to serve it. Seeing that a neighboring vendor was selling waffle cookies, Hamwi took a cookie and rolled it into a cone for holding ice cream. An immediate success, Hamwi's invention was hailed by vendors as a "cornucopia"—an exotic word for a "cone."

STATE WITH THE MOST
T.rex specimens

The first *Tyrannosaurus rex* fossil ever found was discovered in Montana—paleontologist Barnum Brown excavated it in the Hell Creek Formation in 1902. Since then, many major *T. rex* finds have been in Montana—from the "Wankel Rex," discovered in 1988, to "Trix," discovered in 2013.

Another *T. rex* fossil was uncovered in Montana in 2016: "Tufts-Love Rex," named for paleontologists Jason Love and Luke Tufts, was found about 20 percent intact at the site in Hell Creek. Today, the Museum of the Rockies in Bozeman, Montana, houses thirteen *T. rex* specimens—more than anywhere else in the world.

MONTANA

STATE WITH THE LARGEST
indoor rain forest

NEBRASKA

The Lied Jungle at Henry Doorly Zoo in Omaha, Nebraska, features three rain-forest habitats: one each from South America, Africa, and Asia. At 123,000 square feet, this indoor rain forest is larger than two football fields. It measures 80 feet tall, making it as tall as an eight-story building. The Lied Jungle opened in 1992 and cost $15 million to create.

Seven waterfalls rank among its spectacular features. Ninety different animal species live here, including saki monkeys, pygmy hippos, and many reptiles and birds. Exotic plant life includes the African sausage tree, the chocolate tree, and rare orchids. The zoo's other major exhibit—the Desert Dome—is the world's largest indoor desert.

STATE THAT PRODUCES
the most gold
NEVADA

Although it has been called the "Silver State" for its silver production, Nevada is also the state that produces the most gold. According to the Nevada Mining Association, Nevada produces more than three-quarters of America's gold and accounts for 5.4 percent of world gold production. Gold can be found in every county of Nevada, although it is not always accessible to casual prospectors. Nevada's Carlin Trend is rich in gold deposits—and is, in fact, the world's second largest gold resource—but the deposits are so finely spread that they require an expensive process to extract the precious mineral.

STATE WITH THE OLDEST skiing club

NEW HAMPSHIRE

Nansen Ski Club, in Milan, New Hampshire, was founded by Norwegian immigrants in 1872, making it the oldest continuously operating skiing club in the United States. When it first opened, the venue only accepted other Scandinavians living in the area, but was then made available to everyone as more skiing enthusiasts began to move into New Hampshire from Quebec, to work in the mills there. For fifty years, the club was home to the largest ski jump east of the Mississippi, and was used for Olympic tryouts.

STATE WITH THE MOST
diners

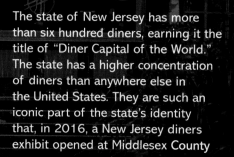

NEW JERSEY

The state of New Jersey has more than six hundred diners, earning it the title of "Diner Capital of the World." The state has a higher concentration of diners than anywhere else in the United States. They are such an iconic part of the state's identity that, in 2016, a New Jersey diners exhibit opened at Middlesex County Museum, showcasing the history of the diner from early twentieth-century lunch cars to modern roadside spots. The state has many different types of diners, including famous restaurant-style eateries like Tops in East Newark, as well as retro hole-in-the-wall diners with jukeboxes and faded booths.

STATE THAT MADE THE WORLD'S LARGEST
flat enchilada

New Mexico was home to the world's largest flat enchilada in October 2014, during the Whole Enchilada Fiesta in Las Cruces. The record-breaking enchilada measured 10.5 feet in diameter and required 250 pounds of masa dough, 175 pounds of cheese, 75 gallons of red chili sauce, 50 pounds of onions, and 175 gallons of oil. Led by Roberto's Mexican Restaurant, the making—and eating—of the giant enchilada was a tradition at the festival for thirty-four years before enchilada master Roberto Estrada hung up his apron in 2015.

NEW MEXICO

America's smallest church

NEW YORK

The smallest church in America, Oneida's Cross Island Chapel, measures 81 by 51 inches and has just enough room for the minister and two churchgoers. Built in 1989, the church is in an odd location, in the middle of a pond. The simple, whitewashed clapboard chapel stands on a little jetty that has moorings for a boat or two. The island that the chapel is named for barely breaks the surface of the water nearby and is simply a craggy pile of rock bearing a cross.

STATE WITH THE LARGEST
private house
NORTH CAROLINA

The Biltmore Estate, in the mountains of Asheville, North Carolina, is home to Biltmore House, the largest privately owned house in the United States. George Vanderbilt commissioned the 250-room French Renaissance–style chateau in 1889, and opened it to his friends and family as a country retreat in 1895. Designed by architect Richard Morris Hunt, Biltmore House has an impressive thirty-five bedrooms and forty-three bathrooms, and boasts a floor space of over four acres. In 1930, the Vanderbilt family opened Biltmore House to the public.

LARGEST PRIVATE ESTATES IN THE USA
Area in square feet

Biltmore Estate, Asheville, NC 175,000

Oheka Castle, Huntington, NY 109,000

Sydell Miller Mansion, Palm Beach, FL 84,626

Pensmore, Highlandville, MO 72,215

Rennert Mansion, Sagaponack, NY, 66,400

BIGGEST honey producer
NORTH DAKOTA

For the last thirteen years, North Dakota has outstripped all other U.S. states in the production of honey. Currently there are 485,000 honey-producing colonies in North Dakota, and in 2016, they produced more than 37.8 million pounds of the sweet stuff. It seems the North Dakota climate is just right for honeybees and—more important—for the flowers from which they collect their nectar. Typical summer weather features warm days but cool nights.

NO SELF RESPECTING WOMA
SHOULD WISH OR WORK
FOR THE SUCC
T
USA B. AN ON

FIRST LAWS protecting
working women
OHIO

In the 1800s, working conditions in U.S. factories were grueling and pay was very low. Most of the workers were women, and it was not uncommon for them to work for twelve to fourteen hours a day, six days a week. The factories were not heated or air-conditioned and there was no compensation for being sick.

By the 1850s, several organizations had formed to improve the working conditions for women and to shorten their workday. In 1852, Ohio passed a law limiting the working day to ten hours for women under the age of eighteen. It was a small step, but it was also the first act of legislation of its kind in the United States.

STATE WITH THE LARGEST
multiple-arch dam
OKLAHOMA

Completed in 1940, the Pensacola Dam in Oklahoma is 6,565 feet long, making it the longest multiple-arch dam in the world. The dam stretches across the Grand River and controls the 43,500 acres of water that form the Grand Lake o' the Cherokees.

The massive structure is a towering 145 feet tall and consists of no fewer than 535,000 cubic yards of concrete, about 655,000 barrels of cement, 75,000 pounds of copper, and a weighty 10 million pounds of structural steel.

STATE WITH THE MOST
photographed
lighthouse
OREGON

Halfway between the towns of Florence and Yachats, Oregon's Heceta Head Lighthouse is the most photographed lighthouse in the United States. Built around 1894, the 205-foot-tall lighthouse is on the National Register of Historic Places, and while the light still works, it is now better known as a romantic bed-and-breakfast location. Heceta Head Lighthouse is famous not just for its beauty—it is also considered one of America's most haunted lighthouses, with stories claiming it is home to a "Gray Lady" called Rue.

the most crayon

PENNSYLVAN

Easton, Pennsylvania, is home to the Crayola crayon factory, and has been the company's headquarters since 1976. The factory produces an amazing twelve million crayons every single day, made from uncolored paraffin and pigment powder.

In 1996, the company opene Crayola Experience in downt Easton. The Experience inclu live interactive show in whic can watch a "crayonologist" crayons, just as they are ma factory nearby.

state stats

STATE WITH THE OLDEST
Fourth of July celebration

RHODE ISLAND

Bristol, Rhode Island, holds America's longest continuously running Fourth of July celebration. The idea for the celebration came from Revolutionary War veteran Rev. Henry Wight, of Bristol's First Congregational Church, who organized "Patriotic Exercises" to honor the nation's founders and those who fought to establish the United States. Today, Bristol begins celebrating the holiday on June 14, and puts on a wide array of events leading up to the Fourth itself—including free concerts, a baseball game, a Fourth of July Ball, and a half marathon.

STATE WITH THE HOTTEST pepper
SOUTH CAROLINA

WORLD'S HOTTEST PEPPERS
By peak heat in millions of SHU

Pepper X 3.18

Dragon's Breath 2.4

Carolina Reaper 2.2

Trinidad Moruga Scorpion 2

Brain Strain 1.9

Pepper X, created by Smokin' Ed Currie of Rock Hill, South Carolina, is the hottest pepper in the world, measuring an average of 3.18 million Scoville heat units (SHU). To get a feel for how hot that is, just know that a regular jalapeño clocks in at 10,000 to 20,000 SHU. Currie also created the world's third-hottest chili, the California Reaper. The Reaper held the record from 2013 to 2017, before being beaten by the 2.4 million SHU Dragon's Breath pepper in May. Just four months after that, Currie's Pepper X took the chili pepper world by storm.

STATE WITH THE LARGEST sculpture

SOUTH DAKOTA

While South Dakota is famous as the home of Mount Rushmore, it is also the location of another giant mountain carving: the Crazy Horse Memorial. The mountain carving, which is still in progress, will be the largest sculpture in the world when it is completed, at 563 feet tall and 641 feet long. Korczak Ziolkowski, who worked on Mount Rushmore, began the carving in 1948 to pay tribute to Crazy Horse—the Lakota Sioux leader who defeated General Custer at the Battle of the Little Bighorn. Nearly seventy years later, Ziolkowski's family continues his work, relying completely on funding from visitors and donors.

STATE THAT MAKES ALL THE
MoonPies
TENNESSEE

Tennessee is the home of the MoonPie, which was conceived there in 1917 by bakery salesman Earl Mitchell Sr. after a group of local miners asked for a filling treat "as big as the moon." Made from marshmallow, graham crackers, and chocolate, the sandwich cookies were soon being mass-produced at Tennessee's Chattanooga Bakery, and MoonPie was registered as a trademark by the bakery in 1919. MoonPies first sold at just five cents each and quickly became popular—even being named the official snack of NASCAR in the late 1990s. Today, Chattanooga Bakery makes nearly a million MoonPies every day.

LARGEST
urban bat
colony
TEXAS

If you want to see a sky filled with hundreds of thousands of bats, head to Austin, Texas, any time from mid-March to November. The city's Ann W. Richards Congress Avenue Bridge is home to the world's largest urban bat colony—roughly 1.5 million bats in all. The Mexican free-tailed bats first settled here in the 1980s, and numbers have grown steadily since. They currently produce around 750,000 pups per year. These days the bats are a tourist attraction that draws about 140,000 visitors to the city, many of them hoping to catch the moment at dusk when large numbers of bats fly out from under the bridge to look for food.

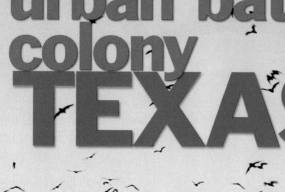

STATE WITH THE LARGEST

saltwater lake
UTAH

The Great Salt Lake, which inspired the name of Utah's largest city, is the largest saltwater lake in the United States, at around 75 miles long and 35 miles wide. Sometimes called "America's Dead Sea," it is typically larger than each of the states of Delaware and Rhode Island. Its size, however, fluctuates as water levels rise and fall: Since 1849, the water level has varied by as much as 20 feet, which can shift the shoreline by up to 15 miles. Great Salt Lake is too salty to support most aquatic life, but is home to several kinds of algae as well as the brine shrimp that feed on them.

STATE THAT
PRODUCES
THE MOST
maple syrup
VERMONT

The state of Vermont produced 1.98 million gallons of maple syrup in 2017, contributing more than 47 percent of the national total. Vermont's more than 1,500 maple syrup producers take sap from 5.41 million tree taps. They have to collect 40 gallons of maple sap in order to produce just 1 gallon of syrup. Producers also use maple sap for making other treats, such as maple butter, sugar, and candies.

STATE WITH THE LARGEST
office building
VIRGINIA

The Pentagon—the headquarters of the United States Department of Defense—is America's largest office building. The five-sided structure, which was completed in 1943 after just sixteen months of work, cost $83 million to build. It contains 3.7 million square feet of office space—and triple the amount of floor space in the Empire State Building—as well as a large central courtyard. Despite containing 17.5 miles of corridors, the building's design means that a person can walk from any point to another in about 7 minutes. There are currently 24,000 employees, both military and civilian, working in the building.

The Teapot Dome Service Station in Zillah, Washington, was once the oldest working gas station in the United States, and is still the only one built to commemorate a political scandal. Now preserved as a museum, the gas station was built in 1922 as a monument to the Teapot Dome Scandal, in which Albert Fall, President Warren G. Harding's secretary of the interior, took bribes to lease government oil reserves to private companies. The gas station, located on Washington's Old Highway 12, was moved in 1978 to make way for Interstate 82, then again in 2007 when it was purchased by the City of Zillah as a historic landmark.

STATE WITH
THE OLDEST
gas station
WASHINGTON

STATE WITH THE LONGEST steel arch bridge
WEST VIRGINIA

The New River Gorge Bridge in Fayetteville spans 3,030 feet and is 876 feet above the New River. It is both the longest and largest steel arch bridge in the United States. Builders used 88 million pounds of steel and concrete to construct it. The $37 million structure took three years to complete and opened on October 22, 1977. Bridge Day, held every October since 1980, is a BASE-jumping event at the New River Gorge Bridge. Hundreds of BASE jumpers and about 80,000 spectators gather for the one-day festival. Among the most popular events is the Big Way, in which large groups of people jump off the bridge together. During Bridge Day 2013, Donald Cripps became one of the world's oldest BASE jumpers, at eighty-four years old.

state stats

LARGEST
cross-country
ski race
WISCONSIN

Each year in February, Wisconsin hosts America's largest cross-country ski race. The race attracts over 10,000 skiers, all attempting to complete the 55-kilometer (34-mile) course from Cable to Hayward. Milestones along the way include Boedecker Hill, Mosquito Brook, and Hatchery Park.

The event is part of the Worldloppet circuit of twenty ski marathons across the globe. The winner of the 2018 race, Benjamin Saxton from Lakeville, Minnesota, completed the course in two hours, forty-seven minutes, and thirty-five seconds to claim the $7,500 prize money.

STATE WITH THE LARGEST
hot spring
WYOMING

Grand Prismatic Spring, in Yellowstone National Park in Wyoming, is the largest hot spring in the United States. The spring measures 370 feet in diameter and is more than 121 feet deep; Yellowstone National Park says that the spring is bigger than a football field and deeper than a ten-story building. Grand Prismatic is not just the largest spring but also the most photographed thermal feature in Yellowstone due to its bright colors. The colors come from different kinds of bacteria, living in each part of the spring, that thrive at various temperatures. As water comes up from the middle of the spring, it is too hot to support most bacterial life, but as the water spreads out to the edges of the spring, it cools in concentric circles.

9

**sports
STARS**

SPORTS STARS
TRENDING#

AROUND THE WORLD IN FORTY-TWO DAYS
Record-breaking solo sailor

In just forty-two days, sixteen hours, forty minutes, and thirty-five seconds, François Gabart of France made a record-breaking solo sail around the world in a trimaran. Sailing from the French port of Brest on November 4, 2017, and arriving at Ouessant, an island off the west coast of France, on December 17, Gabart beat the existing record by more than six days. Jubilant team members used Twitter to announce that Gabart had completed his course.

#MUSLIMWOMENATHLETES
Nike's Pro Hijab

A hijab is a head covering that many Muslim women wear in public for religious reasons—even when competing in sporting competitions. To make life easier, and more comfortable, Nike launched the Pro Hijab in 2017. Made from lightweight, breathable fabric, the garment gets the thumbs-up from Manal Rostom, the first Egyptian woman to run the Great Wall Marathon and the first woman wearing a hijab to feature in an international Nike campaign.

PERFORMANCE BOOSTER
Adidas Futurecraft 4D

In December 2017, leading sportswear brand Adidas launched its Futurecraft 4D range of sneakers, designed to enhance the wearer's performance. Harnessing the technology of 3-D printing, Adidas worked on the most macro scale to fine-tune the midsole millimeter by millimeter to make it perfect in terms of shape, size, and flexibility.

GOING THE DISTANCE
The farthest a woman has ever cycled in one year

In May 2017, U.S. cyclist Amanda Coker made history after completing a year-long cycle ride. She traveled 86,573.2 miles in total—a world record for the greatest distance ever cycled in a year by a woman, according to the World UltraCycling Association. Amazingly, Coker beat the previous record of 29,603.7 miles after just 130 days.

MONSTER JAM SENSATION
Front flip wows crowds

In March 2017, monster-truck driver Lee O'Donnell made history at the Monster Jam World Finals XVIII in Las Vegas, Nevada, when he completed the first-ever front flip the competition has seen. Sitting behind the wheel of his blue truck, nicknamed The Mad Scientist, O'Donnell approached a dirt hill with front wheels raised in the air. The back wheel caught the mound, sending the truck summersaulting into the air before landing squarely on all four tires.

HIGHEST BASE jump from a building

FRED FUGEN AND VINCE REFFET

BASE jumping is just about the world's most terrifying sport to watch. BASE stands for the types of places a person may jump from: Buildings, Antennae, Spans (usually bridges), and Earth (usually cliffs). In April 2014, French daredevils Fred Fugen and Vince Reffet set a new record by jumping from a specially built platform at the top of the world's tallest building, the Burj Khalifa in Dubai. They jumped from a height of 2,716 feet, 6 inches. The highest ever BASE jump was performed by Russian Valery Rozov from 23,690 feet high on the north side of Mount Everest. He landed safely on the Rongbuk Glacier at an altitude of 19,520 feet, some 4,100 feet below.

HIGHEST
basketball shot

HOW
RIDICULOUS

Australian trick-shot group How Ridiculous continues to break its own record. In 2015 one member made a basket from an amazing 415 feet, but the group has since improved that distance several times. In January 2018 How Ridiculous achieved its most astonishing feat yet: a basket from 660 feet, 10 inches. The group made the record shot at Maletsunyane Falls, Lesotho, in southern Africa, after five days of setup work

and practice. How Ridiculous is a group of three friends who started trying trick shots for fun in their backyards in 2009. They now have a successful YouTube channel and business and are also involved in Christian charitable work.

LONGEST
skateboard
ramp jump
DANNY
WAY

Many extreme sports activities are showcased at the annual X Games and Winter X Games. At the 2004 X Games, held in Los Angeles, skateboarder Danny Way set an amazing record that remains unbeaten. On June 19, Way made a long-distance jump of 79 feet, beating his own 2003 world record (75 feet). In 2005 he jumped over the Great Wall of China. He made the jump despite having torn ligaments in his ankle during a practice jump on the previous day.

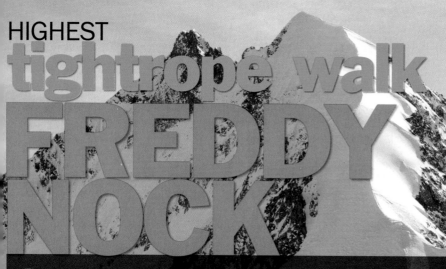

HIGHEST
tightrope walk
FREDDY NOCK

Tightrope walking looks hard enough a few feet above the ground, but Swiss stuntman Freddy Nock took it to the next level when he walked between two mountains in the Swiss Alps in March 2015. On a rope set 11,590 feet above sea level, Freddy took about thirty-nine minutes to walk the 1,140 feet across to the neighboring peak. The previous record had held since 1974, when Frenchman Philippe Petit walked between the Twin Towers of New York's former World Trade Center.

HIGHEST-SCORING
NBA game
DETROIT PISTONS VS. DENVER NUGGETS
1983

The Detroit Pistons and the Denver Nuggets played this game in Denver on December 13, 1983. The game went to three overtime periods before the Pistons won 186–184, scoring 33 more points than the next-highest-scoring match (Spurs vs. Bucks, March 1982).

The Pistons' 186 points mark the highest total ever scored by a team. The losing team, Denver, also lost in the highest-scoring game without overtime: 162–158 points, won by the Golden State Warriors in November 1990.

HIGHEST-SCORING NBA GAMES
Total points scored (final score)

Game	Score
Detroit Pistons vs. Denver Nuggets	370 (186–184) December 1983
San Antonio Spurs vs. Milwaukee Bucks	337 (171–166) March 1982
Golden State Warriors vs. Denver Nuggets	320 (162–158) November 1990
Denver Nuggets vs. San Antonio Spurs	318 (163–155) January 1984
Phoenix Suns vs. New Jersey Nets*	318 (161–157) December 2006

* This team is now known as the Brooklyn Nets

NBA team
WITH THE MOST CHAMPIONSHIP TITLES
BOSTON CELTICS

The Boston Celtics top the NBA winners' list with seventeen championship titles out of twenty-one appearances in the finals, just one title more than the Los Angeles Lakers. The two teams have met twelve times in the finals, resulting in nine wins for the Celtics. The best years for the Boston Celtics were the 1960s, with 1967 being the only year in the decade that they did not bring the championship home.

NBA CHAMPIONSHIP WINS

Boston Celtics	17	1957–2008
LA Lakers	16	1949–2010
Golden State Warriors	6	1947–2018
Chicago Bulls	6	1991–1998
San Antonio Spurs	5	1999–2014

MOST CAREER POINTS

in the NBA
KAREEM ABDUL-JABBAR

Many fans regard Abdul-Jabbar as the greatest-ever basketball player. Abdul-Jabbar was known by his birth name, Lew Alcindor, until 1971, when he changed his name after converting to Islam. That same year he led the Milwaukee Bucks to the team's first NBA championship title. As well as being the all-time highest scorer of points during his professional career with a total of 38,387, Abdul-Jabbar also won the NBA Most Valuable Player (MVP) award a record six times.

NBA MOST CAREER POINTS LEADERS
Number of points

Kareem Abdul-Jabbar	38,387
Karl Malone	36,928
Kobe Bryant	33,643
Michael Jordan	32,292
Wilt Chamberlain	31,419

YOUNGEST
NBA PLAYER
to reach
30,000
career
points
LEBRON
JAMES

On Tuesday, January 23, 2018, at the age of thirty-three years and twenty-four days, LeBron James became the youngest player in NBA history to reach 30,000 points, smashing Kobe Bryant's previous record by more than a year. On top of building his own scoring record, James also works hard for his team. In February 2018 he became the first player to reach 30,000 points, 8,000 assists, and 8,000 rebounds. James may even challenge Kareem Abdul-Jabbar in the career-points table before he retires.

DIANA TAURASI

WNBA PLAYER WITH THE MOST career points

MOST CAREER POINTS IN THE WNBA
Number of points

Diana Taurasi	7,867
Tina Thompson	7,488
Tamika Catchings	7,380
Cappie Pondexter	6,591
Katie Smith	6,452

After a standout college career and three NCAA championships with the University of Connecticut Huskies, Diana Taurasi joined the Phoenix Mercury in the WNBA in 2004. Her prolific scoring helped the Mercury to their first WNBA title in 2007 (and two more since then) and her international career includes four consecutive Team USA Olympic golds, 2004–16. Playing mainly as guard, Taurasi became the all-time leading WNBA scorer in 2017.

MOST SUCCESSFUL NCAA basketball coach ever

PAT SUMMITT

Patricia "Pat" Summitt won 1,098 NCAA games as head coach of the University of Tennessee Lady Volunteers from 1974 to 2012, more than any other coach. Acclaimed as Naismith Coach of the Century in 2000, she also had a notable playing career, winning an Olympic silver medal as co-captain of the USA women's team in 1976.

When Summitt started coaching the Lady Vols in 1974, the first NCAA women's basketball championship was still eight years in the future. Her teams eventually won eight NCAA national titles, and in thirty-eight years as a coach, she never had a losing season. Ms. Summitt died of Alzheimer's disease in 2016, yet her impressive legacy lives on.

273

MOST VALUABLE
football team
DALLAS
COWBOYS

It has been nore than twenty years since the Dallas Cowboys won the Super Bowl, yet the team has been the most valuable in the NFL for eleven straight seasons up to 2017. The team was most recently valued at $4.8 billion. Cowboys' owner Jerry Jones paid what now seems a bargain $150 million for the franchise in 1989. In recent years broadcast and stadium revenues in the NFL have soared.

NFL TEAM VALUATIONS
Revenue in billions of U.S. dollars
September 2017

Dallas Cowboys	4.8
New England Patriots	3.7
New York Giants	3.3
Washington Redskins	3.1
San Francisco 49ers	3.05

NFL PLAYER WITH THE MOST
career touchdowns
JERRY RICE

Jerry Rice is generally regarded as the greatest wide receiver in NFL history. He played in the NFL for twenty seasons—fifteen of them with the San Francisco 49ers—and won three Super Bowl rings. As well as leading the career touchdowns list with 208, Rice also holds the "most yards gained" mark with 23,546 yards. Most of his touchdowns were from pass receptions (197), often working with the great 49ers quarterback Joe Montana.

NFL PLAYERS WITH THE MOST CAREER TOUCHDOWNS
Number of touchdowns (career years)

Player	Touchdowns	Career years
Jerry Rice	208	1985–2004
Emmitt Smith	175	1990–2004
LaDainian Tomlinson	162	2001–2011
Terrell Owens	156	1996–2010
Randy Moss	156	1998–2012

NFL PLAYER WITH THE MOST
pass completions
BRETT FAVRE

NFL PLAYERS WITH THE MOST PASS COMPLETIONS
Number of completions (career years)

Brett Favre	6,300	1991–2010
Drew Brees	6,222	2001–2017
Peyton Manning	6,125	1988–2015
Tom Brady	5,629	2000–2017
Dan Marino	4,967	1983–1999

After playing as a rookie with the Atlanta Falcons, Brett Favre moved to the Green Bay Packers, then the New York Jets and the Minnesota Vikings. In eighteen of his twenty seasons with these teams, he passed for more than 3,000 yards. Favre, also known as "The Gunslinger," beat all other NFL players for career regular season passes completed. He also led the Packers to victory in Super Bowl XXXI, passing for two touchdowns and scoring a third himself.

NFL TEAM WITH THE MOST
Super Bowl wins
PITTSBURGH STEELERS

Although the Pittsburgh Steelers (founded in 1933 as the Pittsburgh Pirates) are one of the oldest pro football teams, they were not very impressive in their early years. Since the 1970s, however, they have compiled one of the best all-around records in the NFL and now top the list with six Super Bowl wins out of eight appearances. The arrival of Chuck Noll as coach in 1969 was their turning point. Noll's teams, made up of such all-time greats as Terry Bradshaw, Franco Harris, and Joe Greene, won back-to-back Super Bowls twice.

NFL TEAMS WITH THE MOST SUPER BOWL WINS
Number of wins

Pittsburgh Steelers	6	Super Bowls IX, X, XIII, XIV, XL, XLIII
San Francisco 49ers	5	Super Bowls XVI, XIX, XXIII, XXIV, XXIX
Dallas Cowboys	5	Super Bowls VI, XII, XXVII, XXVIII, XXX
New England Patriots	5	Super Bowls XXXVI, XXXVIII, XXXIX, XLIX, LI
Green Bay Packers	4	Super Bowls I, II, XXXI, XLV
New York Giants	4	Super Bowls XXI, XXV, XLII, XLVI

school with most Rose Bowl wins

The Rose Bowl is college football's oldest postseason event, first played in 1902. Taking place near January 1 of each year, the game is normally played between the Pac-12 Conference champion and the Big Ten Conference champion, but one year in three is part of college football's playoffs.

The University of Southern California has easily the best record in the Rose Bowl, with twenty-five wins from thirty-four appearances, followed by the Michigan Wolverines (eight wins from twenty). The Georgia Bulldogs defeated the Oklahoma Sooners 54–48 in the 2018 game but lost the College Football Playoff National Championship to the Alabama Crimson Tide a week later.

USC TROJANS

World Series wins

NEW YORK YANKEES

WORLD SERIES WINS
Number of wins

New York Yankees	27	1923–2009
St. Louis Cardinals	11	1926–2011
Oakland Athletics*	9	1910–1989
San Francisco Giants**	8	1905–2014
Boston Red Sox***	8	1903–2013

* Previously played in Kansas City and Philadelphia

** Previously played in New York

*** Originally Boston Americans

The New York Yankees are far and away the most successful team in World Series history. Since baseball's championship was first contested in 1903, the Yankees have appeared forty times and won on twenty-seven occasions. The Yankees' greatest years were from the 1930s through the 1950s, when the team was led by legends like Babe Ruth and Joe DiMaggio. Nearest challengers are the St. Louis Cardinals from the National League with eleven wins from nineteen appearances.

MLB TEAM WITH THE HIGHEST

salary LOS ANGELES DODGERS

Major League Baseball has no team salary cap, and as revenues from television and other sources have increased in recent years player salaries have risen accordingly. For the 2017 season the Los Angeles Dodgers were yet again the highest-paying club, with a player salary bill of around $227.8 million. This included baseball's top earner, pitcher Clayton Kershaw, who earned $33 million. Despite their high-value players the Dodgers were defeated by the Houston Astros in the 2017 World Series.

The 2016 World Series saw a dramatic showdown between the two Major League Baseball clubs with the longest World Series droughts: the Chicago Cubs and the Cleveland Indians. The Cubs had been one of baseball's most successful teams in the early years of the World Series at the start of the twentieth century, but between 1908 and 1945, they lost the World Series seven times. Following that string of World Series losses, the team scarcely won even a divisional title until 2016—the year the drought finally ended. The Cubs clinched the World Series title in the tenth inning in the deciding seventh game.

CHICAGO CUBS,
BROKEN 2016

WORLD SERIES DROUGHTS

Team	Last World Series win	Last appearance in World Series
Cleveland Indians	1948	2016
Texas Rangers	Never (since 1961*)	2011
Milwaukee Brewers	Never (since 1969*)	1982
San Diego Padres	Never (since 1969*)	1998
Washington Nationals	Never (since 1969*)	Never

* Dates when the teams were established

MLB PLAYER WITH THE HIGHEST
batting average

HIGHEST CAREER BATTING AVERAGES
Batting average (career years)

Ty Cobb	.366	1905–1928
Rogers Hornsby	.359	1915–1937
Shoeless Joe Jackson	.356	1908–1920
Lefty O'Doul	.349	1919–1934
Ed Delahanty	.346	1888–1903

TY COBB

Ty Cobb's batting average of .366 is one of the longest-lasting records in Major League Baseball. In reaching that mark, Cobb, known to fans as "The Georgia Peach," astonishingly batted .300 or better in twenty-three consecutive seasons, mainly with the Detroit Tigers. Cobb's status in the game was made clear when he easily topped the selection poll for the first set of inductees into the Baseball Hall of Fame.

MLB PLAYER WITH THE MOST home runs

CAREER HOME RUNS
Number of home runs (career years)

Barry Bonds	762	1986–2007
Hank Aaron	755	1954–1976
Babe Ruth	714	1914–1935
Alex Rodriguez	696	1994–2016
Willie Mays	660	1951–1973

Barry Bonds's power hitting and skill in the outfield rank him as a five-tool player—someone with good speed and baserunning skills, who is also good at hitting the ball, fielding, and throwing. He played his first seven seasons with the Pittsburgh Pirates before moving to the San Francisco Giants for the next twelve seasons. He not only holds the record for most career home runs, but also for the single-season record of seventy-three home runs, which was set in 2001. Barry's godfather is Willie Mays, the first player ever to hit 300 career home runs and steal 300 bases.

BARRY BONDS

BECK
47

MLS PLAYER WITH THE MOST
regular-season goals

LANDON DONOVAN

Landon Donovan is Major League Soccer's all-time top scorer. After coming out of retirement for the 2016 season, Donovan now has 144 regular-season goals and 136 assists—again the record mark. In addition, Donovan holds the goal-scoring record for the U.S. national team, with 57 from 157 appearances. Donovan played for LA Galaxy for most of his career, but also appeared and scored in the German Bundesliga and the English Premier League.

MLS REGULAR-SEASON TOP SCORERS
Number of goals (career years)

Landon Donovan	144	2001–2016
Jeff Cunningham	134	1998–2011
Chris Wondolowski	134	2005–
Jaime Moreno	133	1996–2010
Ante Razov	114	1996–2009

COUNTRY WITH THE MOST
FIFA World
Cup wins
BRAZIL

Brazil, host of the 2014 FIFA World Cup, has lifted the trophy the most times in the tournament's history. Second on the list, Germany, has more runners-up and semifinal appearances and hence, arguably, a stronger record overall. However, many would say that Brazil's 1970 lineup, led by the incomparable Pelé, ranks as the finest team ever. The host team has won five of the twenty tournaments that have been completed to date.

FIFA WORLD CUP WINNERS
Number of wins

Brazil	5	1958, 1962, 1970, 1994, 2002
Germany*	4	1954, 1974, 1990, 2014
Italy	4	1934, 1938 1982, 2006
Argentina	2	1978, 1986
Uruguay	2	1930, 1950

Three teams have won the tournament once (England 1966, France 1988, Spain 2010).

* As West Germany 1954, 1974

COUNTRY WITH THE MOST
FIFA Women's World Cup wins

Fan Yunjie

Kristine Lilly

UNITED STATES

In 1991, the first Women's World Cup was held, in which the USA beat Norway 2–1 in the final. Since then, the United States has won the tournament twice more and has gained second or third place on every other occasion. Soccer legend Kristine Lilly was on the winning team in 1991, and again when the United States won in 1999. She competed in five World Cup tournaments in total.

FIFA WOMEN'S WORLD CUP WINNERS
Number of wins

United States	3	1991, 1999, 2015
Germany	2	2003, 2007
Norway	1	1995
Japan	1	2011

KRISTINE LILLY

WOMAN WITH THE MOST international soccer caps

In her long and successful career, Kristine Lilly has played her club soccer principally with the Boston Breakers. When she made her debut on the U.S. national team in 1987, however, she was still in high school. Her total of 354 international caps is the world's highest for a man or woman and her trophy haul includes two World Cup winner's medals and two Olympic golds.

WOMEN WITH THE MOST INTERNATIONAL SOCCER CAPS
Number of caps (career years)

Kristine Lilly, USA	354	1987–2010
Christie Rampone, USA	311	1997–2015
Mia Hamm, USA	276	1987–2004
Julie Foudy, USA	272	1988–2004
Christine Sinclair, Canada	268	2000–

LOWEST WINNING SCORE
in a major golf tournament

In Gee Chun of South Korea is still in the early stages of her professional career but has already achieved two wins in the five annual women's golf "majors." Most remarkable of all was her achievement at the 2016 Evian Championship: the lowest score in a major championship by any player, male or female, at twenty-one under par. The previous women's record was nineteen under par, shared by five players, while two players share the men's record of twenty under par.

IN GEE CHUN

PGA GOLFER WITH LOWEST season average 2017

Texas-born Jordan Spieth had a great season in 2017, winning the prestigious Vardon Trophy and Byron Nelson Award for the lowest scoring average in PGA golf. Spieth averaged 68.85 shots per round in a season that included two PGA Tour wins as well as his third success in a major, when he won the British Open at Royal Birkdale. Spieth's best season to date has been 2015, when he won two majors, topped the money list, and claimed both scoring-average titles.

WOMAN WITH THE MOST
Grand Slam titles
MARGARET COURT

The Grand Slam tournaments are the four most important tennis events of the year: the Australian Open; the French Open; Wimbledon; and the U.S. Open. The dominant force in women's tennis throughout the 1960s and into the 1970s, Australia's Margaret Court heads the all-time singles list with twenty-four, although Serena Williams may beat this. Court won an amazing sixty-four Grand Slam titles in singles, women's doubles, and mixed doubles, a total that seems unlikely to be beaten.

TOTAL GRAND SLAM TITLES
Number of titles (singles) (years active)

Margaret Court, Australia	64 (24)	1960–1975
Martina Navratilova, Czech/USA	59 (18)	1974–2006
Serena Williams, USA	39 (23)	1998–
Billie Jean King, USA	39 (12)	1961–1980
Margaret Osborne duPont, USA	37 (6)	1941–1962

ROGER FEDERER

MAN WITH THE MOST
Grand Slam singles titles

With twenty wins, Swiss tennis star Roger Federer stands at the top of the all-time rankings in Grand Slam tennis singles tournaments. His best tournament has been Wimbledon, which he has won eight times. Federer, did not win a Grand Slam between 2012 and 2017, partly due to injury troubles. In 2017, however, after a break for knee surgery, he was back and as good as ever, with wins in Australia (repeated in 2018) and at Wimbledon.

GRAND SLAM SINGLES WINS
Number of wins (years active)

Roger Federer, Switzerland	20	1998–
Rafael Nadal, Spain	17	2001–
Pete Sampras, USA	14	1988–2002
Roy Emerson, Australia	12	1961–1973
Novak Djokovic, Serbia	12	2003–

MOST CONSECUTIVE
NASCAR
championship wins

JIMMIE
JOHNSON

Now officially the Monster Energy NASCAR Cup Series, the NASCAR drivers' championship has been contested since 1949. California native Jimmie Johnson is tied at the top of the all-time wins list with seven, but his five-season streak, 2006–10, is easily the best in the sport's history. Johnson's racing career began on 50cc motorcycles when he was just five years old. All of Johnson's NASCAR championship wins have been achieved driving Chevrolets; his current car is a Camaro ZL1. He has won eighty-three NASCAR races so far in his career but surely has more to come.

NASCAR CHAMPIONSHIP WINS
Number of wins (years in which the title was won)

Jimmie Johnson	7 (2006, 2007, 2008, 2009, 2010, 2013, 2016)
Dale Earnhardt Sr.	7 (1980, 1986, 1987, 1990, 1991, 1993, 1994)
Richard Petty	7 (1964, 1967, 1971, 1972, 1974, 1975, 1979)
Jeff Gordon	4 (1995, 1997, 1998, 2001)

Triple Crown wins

EDDIE ARCARO

Many horse-racing experts think that Eddie Arcaro was the best-ever American jockey. Arcaro rode his first winner in 1932, and by the time of his retirement thirty years later, he had won the Triple Crown twice, in 1941 and 1948. He also won more Triple Crown races than any other jockey, although Bill Hartack has equaled Arcaro's total of five successes in the Kentucky Derby. Arcaro won 4,779 races overall in his career.

JOCKEYS WITH MULTIPLE WINS IN TRIPLE CROWN RACES
Number of wins (years active)

Eddie Arcaro	17	1938–1957
Bill Shoemaker	11	1955–1986
Earl Sande	9	1921–1930
Bill Hartack	9	1956–1969
Pat Day	9	1985–2000
Gary Stevens	9	1988–2013

NHL TEAM WITH THE MOST
Stanley Cup wins

The Montreal Canadiens are the oldest and, by far, the most successful National Hockey League team. In its earliest years, the Stanley Cup had various formats, but since 1927, it has been awarded exclusively to the champion NHL team—and the Canadiens have won it roughly one year in every four. Their most successful years were the 1940s through the 1970s, when the team was inspired by all-time greats like Maurice Richard and Guy Lafleur.

STANLEY CUP WINNERS (SINCE 1915)
Number of wins (time span)

Montreal Canadiens	24	1916–1993
Toronto Maple Leafs	11	1918–1967
Detroit Red Wings	11	1936–2008
Boston Bruins	6	1929–2011
Chicago Blackhawks	6	1934–2015

MONTREAL CANADIENS

JONATHAN TOEWS

HIGHEST-PAID NHL player

The Chicago Blackhawks' Jonathan Toews was the NHL's highest-paid player for the 2017–18 season—between salary and endorsements, Toews earned a reported total of $16 million. In 2014, Toews and teammate Patrick Kane signed matching deals with the Blackhawks earning them each $84 million over eight years. Toews was the Blackhawks' youngest-ever team captain when appointed in 2008, and has since led the team to three Stanley Cup wins in six years, including the Blackhawks' first win since 1961. Toews is the youngest member of the "Triple Gold Club," having won a Stanley Cup, World Championship gold, and an Olympic gold medal by age twenty-two. Only twenty-seven players in history have achieved all three victories.

NHL PLAYER WITH THE MOST
career
points

WAYNE
GRETZKY

Often called "The Great One," Wayne Gretzky is regarded as the most successful hockey player. As well as scoring more goals and assists than any other NHL player—both in regular-season and in postseason games—Gretzky held over sixty NHL records in all by the time of his retirement in 1999. The majority of these records still stand. Although he was unusually small for an NHL player, Gretzky had great skills and an uncanny ability to be in the right place at the right time.

NHL ALL-TIME HIGHEST
REGULAR-SEASON SCORERS
Number of points (goals) (career years)

Wayne Gretzky	2,857 (894)	1978–1999
Jaromír Jágr	1,921 (766)	1990–
Mark Messier	1,887 (694)	1979–2004
Gordie Howe	1,850 (801)	1946–1979
Ron Francis	1,798 (549)	1981–2004

YOUGEST-EVER NHL captain

CONNOR MCDAVID

At nineteen years old, center Connor McDavid was named team captain of the Edmonton Oilers at the beginning of the 2016–17 season. Remarkably, the season before that was his first in the NHL. McDavid has been hailed as the "Next One" (hockey's next household name). His value to the Oilers was made plain in 2017 when he signed a record $100 million, eight-year contract, to begin in 2018–19.

FIRST
WOMAN
TO PLAY
in an NHL game

MANON RHÉAUME

Manon Rhéaume had a fine career as a goaltender in women's ice hockey, earning World Championship gold medals with the Canadian National Women's Team. She is also the first—and only—woman to play for an NHL club. On September 23, 1992, she played one period for the Tampa Bay Lightning in an exhibition game against the St. Louis Blues, during which she saved seven of nine shots. She later played twenty-four games for various men's teams in the professional International Hockey League.

FASTEST
spin on ice skates
OLIVIA RYBICKA-OLIVER

Although only eleven years old at the time of her record-breaking performance, Olivia Rybicka-Oliver from Nova Scotia, Canada, achieved an astonishing spin rate of 342 revolutions per minute—over five per second. This smashed the previous record of 308 revolutions per minute.

Olivia, who is Polish by birth, set her record in Warsaw on January 19, 2015. Her performance was part of a fund-raising event held by Poland's Fundacja Dziecięca Fantazja (Children's Fantasy Foundation) for terminally ill children.

299

FIRST-EVER SKATER

to land six quadruple jumps

NATHAN CHEN

Nathan Chen made skating history at the 2018 Winter Olympics by being the first-ever skater to attempt and land six quadruple jumps during one performance. Quad jumps—in which the skater spins around four times while in the air—are among the hardest moves in skating, and grouping several of them in one program makes them more difficult still. Chen's record-breaking Olympic performance did not earn him a medal because he had skated poorly earlier in the competition, but a few weeks later he won the World Championship after landing his six quads once again.

MOST MEDALS
won by a nation in one Summer Olympics
USA

The record medal count of 239 (including 78 golds) has been held by the United States since the 1904 Games in St. Louis, Missouri. In those days, international travel was much more difficult than it is now—as a result, it's estimated that about 90 percent of the competitors were Americans! Just twelve countries competed and only ten countries won any medals. By comparison, 206 countries competed at Rio 2016.

MOST MEDALS won by an individual

MICHAEL PHELPS

Michael Phelps may be the greatest competitive swimmer ever. He did not win any medals at his first Olympics in 2000, but at each of the Summer Games from 2004 through 2016 he was the most successful individual athlete of any nation. When he announced his retirement after London 2012, he was already the most decorated Olympic athlete ever—but he didn't stay retired for long. At Rio 2016 he won five more golds and a silver, taking his medal total to twenty-eight—twenty-three of them gold.

MOST SUCCESSFUL OLYMPIANS
Number of medals won (gold)

Michael Phelps	USA	Swimming	2004–16	28 (23)
Larisa Latynina	USSR	Gymnastics	1956–64	18 (9)
Nikolai Andrianov	USSR	Gymnastics	1972–80	15 (7)

Four athletes, Ole Einar Bjørndalen of Norway, Boris Shakhlin of the Soviet Union, Edoardo Mangiarotti of Italy, and Takashi Ono of Japan, have each won thirteen medals.

MOST DECORATED
American gymnast ever

Although she was only nineteen during the Rio Olympics, Simone Biles's four gold medals and one bronze took her medal tally from world championships and Olympics to nineteen, a new American record. Biles is only four foot eight, but her tiny frame is full of power and grace, displayed most memorably in her favorite floor exercise discipline. Perhaps the only glitch in her career so far was when a bee chased her off the podium when she was being awarded her 2014 World All-Around gold medal.

SIMONE
BILES

Rio2016 ⭕⭕⭕⭕⭕

Jamaica's Usain Bolt is the greatest track sprinter who has ever lived. Other brilliant Olympic finalists have described how all they can do is watch as he almost disappears into the distance. Usain's greatest victories have been his triple Olympic gold medals at London 2012 and Rio 2016, plus two golds from Beijing 2008. He holds the 100 meter world record (9.58s) and the 200 meter record (19.19s), both from the 2009 World Championships.

FASTEST
man in the world
USAIN
BOLT

FASTEST 100-METER SPRINTS OF ALL TIME
Time in seconds

Usain Bolt (Jamaica) 9.58 Berlin 2009

Usain Bolt (Jamaica) 9.63 London 2012

Usain Bolt (Jamaica) 9.69 Beijing 2008

Tyson Gay (USA) 9.69 Shanghai 2009

Yohan Blake (Jamaica) 9.69 Lausanne 2012

MOST DECORATED
Paralympian ever
TRISCHA ZORN

Trischa Zorn is the most successful Paralympian of all time, having won an astonishing fifty-five medals, forty-one of them gold, at the Paralympic Games from 1980 to 2000. She won every Paralympic event she entered from 1980 to 1988. Zorn is blind and helps disabled military veterans enter the world of parasport. Zorn was inducted into the Paralympic Hall of Fame in 2012.

LEADING FEMALE PARALYMPIC MEDALISTS
Number of medals won

Trischa Zorn, USA 55

Beatrice Hess, France 25

Sarah Storey, Great Britain 25

Chantal Petitclerc, Canada 21

Mayumi Narita, Japan 20

COUNTRY WITH THE MOST
all-time Paralympic medals
USA

Although China topped the Paralympic medal table at the 2016 Summer Games in Rio (239 medals), with the United States coming in fourth (115 medals), the United States comfortably leads the all-time medal count in the Paralympic Summer Games. Norway heads the standings in the Winter Games, with the United States in second, giving the United States an overall medal total that will be unbeatable for many years to come.

COUNTRY WITH THE MOST PARALYMPIC MEDALS
Total number of medals won

United States	2,494
Germany*	1,871
Great Britain	1,824
Canada	1,220
France	1,209

*includes totals of former East and West Germany

FIRST
Paralympic
triathlon
RIO 2016

Most people would find a 750-meter swim, followed by a 20-kilometer bike ride, then a 5-kilometer run quite challenging—but then try all that with a physical or visual impairment, too. That's how it is for paratriathletes. Sixty Paralympians qualified for the first-ever Olympic paratriathlon at Rio in 2016. Only six of the possible ten events (men and women) were contested in Rio, with the United States' two golds, one silver, and one bronze being the best national result.

index

Photo credits

Photos ©: cover top left: AF archive/Alamy Stock Photo; cover top right: Ferrari/ZUMA Press/Newscom; cover center: Joe McNally/Getty Images; cover bottom left: Lifestyle pictures/Alamy Stock Photo; cover bottom center: Larry Busacca/PW/Getty Images; cover bottom right: Editorial/Alamy Stock Photo; cover background and throughout: -strizh-/

Shutterstock; back cover top left: BFA/Alamy Stock Photo; back cover top right: Marco Bertorello/AFP/Getty Images; back cover bottom left: The Photo Access/Alamy Stock Photo; back cover bottom right: Brandon Cole Marine Photography; 4-5: yakub88/Shutterstock; 6 top: Photoshot/Avalon; 6 bottom: Charles Sykes/AP Images; 7 top: Science & Society

Picture Library/Getty Images; 7 center: Media Union/
Shutterstock; 7 center mask: tassel78/Shutterstock;
7 bottom: Christopher Polk/Getty Images; 8: Isabel
Infantes/AP Images; 9: Pawel Supernak/EPA/
Shutterstock; 10: John Shearer/Getty Images; 11:
Steve Russell/Getty Images; 12: Jonathan Short/AP
Images; 13: Chelsea Lauren/Shutterstock; 14:
Associated Press/AP Images; 14 record icons:
mara_lingstad/iStockphoto; 15: George Pimentel/
Wirelmage; 16: Jose Mendez/EPA-EFE/Shutterstock;
17: Kevork Djansezian/Getty Images; 18: Kevin
Mazur/GettyImages; 19: Christopher Polk/Getty
Images; 20: R. Diamond/Getty Images; 21: Kevin
Mazur/Getty Images; 22: Mindy Small/Getty Images;
23: Scott Legato/Getty Images; 24-25: AF archive/
Alamy Stock Photo; 26 top: Chelsea Lauren/
Shutterstock; 26 bottom: Lifestyle pictures/Alamy
Stock Photo; 27 top: Chris Pizzello/AP Images; 27
center: NBC/Getty Images; 27 bottom: Casey Curry/
AP Images; 28: FOX/Getty Images; 28 background:
zaricm/iStockphoto; 29: NBC/Getty Images; 30:
Austin Nelson/BFA/Shutterstock; 31: Mark J. Terrill/
AP Images; 32: George Gojkovich/Getty Images; 33:
CBS Photo Archive/Getty Images; 34 camera icons:
Anthonycz/iStockphoto; 34-35: Pictorial Press Ltd/
Alamy Stock Photo; 36: BFA/Alamy Stock Photo; 37
oscar icons: Samtoon/iStockphoto; 38: Gabriel
Olsen/Getty Images; 39: AF archive/Alamy Stock
Photo; 40-41: Moviestore collection Ltd/Alamy Stock
Photo; 42 left: Featureflash/Dreamstime; 42 right:
Andrea Raffin/Shutterstock; 43: Matt Sayles/AP
Images; 44: Swan Gallet/WWD/Shutterstock; 45: Ken
McKay/ITV/Shutterstock; 46: David M. Benett/Getty
Images; 47: Photo 12/Alamy Stock Photo; 48: Simon
Fergusson/Getty Images; 48 mask icons: Panptys/
iStockphoto; 49: China Photos/Getty Images; 50:
Bruce Glikas/Getty Images; 51: Nick Harvey/Getty
Images; 52-53: Xinhua/Alamy Stock Photo; 54 top:
NASA; 54 bottom: Rich Polk/Getty Images; 55 top:
Ollie Millington/Getty Images; 55 top background:
NCS Production/Shutterstock; 55 center: Mladen
Antonov/AFP/Getty Images; 55 bottom: Car Culture,
Inc./Getty Images; 56: Jeff Greenberg/Getty Images;
57: Ethan Miller/Getty Images; 58: Tim DeFrisco/
Getty Images; 59: Jonathan Hordle/Shutterstock; 60:
David Taylor/Allsport/Getty Images; 61: VCG/Getty
Images; 62: Anadolu Agency/Getty Images; 63:
PHOTOPQR/Ouest France/MAXPPP/Newscom; 64:
Tony Gutierrez/AP Images; 65 top: Les Cunliffe/
Dreamstime; 65 bottom: Courtesy of Pima Air &
Space Museum; 66, 67, 68-69: NASA; 70: Iain
Masterton/age fotostock; 71: Schlitterbahn
Waterparks and Resorts; 72: tintin75/iStockphoto;
73: Ted S. Warren/AP Images; 74-75: NithidPhoto/
iStockphoto; 76 top: Kasto80/Dreamstime; 76
bottom: SeaRick1/Shutterstock; 77 top: dbimages/
Alamy Stock Photo; 77 center: Riccardo Giordano
fotosicki/IP/Shutterstock; 77 bottom: ThyssenKrupp/
Cover Images/Newscom; 78: samxmeg/iStockphoto;
79: Daniel Gustafson/Getty Images; 80: Courtesy of
AirplaneHome.com; 81: bubaone/iStockphoto; 81
car: CSA Images/B&W Icon Collection/Getty Images;
81 background: funnybank/iStockphoto; 82: Splash

News/HotelPresidentWilson/Newscom; 83: Courtesy
of Palacio de Sal Hotel; 84-85: Jon Arnold/Getty
Images; 86: Beercates/Dreamstime; 87: Crystal
Lagoons/Shutterstock; 88: Jae S. Lee/AP Images; 89:
fazon1/iStockphoto; 90: bluehand/Shutterstock; 90
red leaves: Solknar/Shutterstock; 91: Regina Usher/
age fotostock; 92-93: Chederros/age fotostock; 94:
Kajanek/Dreamstime; 95: David Davies/Alamy Stock
Photo; 96: Jack Guez/AFP/Getty Images; 97: Sylvain
Grandadam/age fotostock; 98-99: Kevork
Djansezian/Getty Images; 100 top: MarianVejcik/
Thinkstock; 100 bottom: Diane Bondareff/AP Images;
101 top: ilbusca/iStockphoto; 101 center: Kim Hong-
ji/Reuters; 101 bottom: Jim Watson/AFP/Getty
Images; 102: C Flanigan/Getty Images; 103: Ellen
DeGeneres/Twitter/Getty Images; 103 phone:
martin-dm/iStockphoto; 104: Bizoon/Dreamstime;
105: Mohamad Faizal Ramli/Dreamstime; 106:
PongsakornJun/Thinkstock; 106 emoticon: Stock
Vector One/Shutterstock; 107: Clasos/Getty Images;
108 bottles: Maxandrew/Dreamstime; 108 thumb
icons: Fantasycreationz/Dreamstime; 109:
Associated Press/AP Images; 110: The Photo
Access/Alamy Stock Photo; 111: Amanda Edwards/
Getty Images; 112: Kevork Djansezian/Getty Images;
113: Courtesy Riot Games; 114: David L. Moore-
Lifestyle/Alamy Stock Photo; 115: Stephen Lam/
Getty Images; 116-117: theodore liasi/Alamy Stock
Photo; 118: NASA; 119: Maximilien Brice/CERN;
120-121: Andreas Muehlbauer, Furth im Wald; 122:
courtesy of CMR Surgical; 123: Courtesy of AJ
Lovering; 124-125: Flip Nicklin/Minden Pictures;
126 top: David Gruber; 126 bottom: Georgina
Goodwin/Barcroft Media/Getty Images; 127 top:
ullstein bild/Getty Images; 127 center: Sandesh
Kadur/Nature Picture Library; 127 bottom: Brian V.
Brown; 128: Marius Sipa/Dreamstime; 129: Nicholas
Bergkessel, Jr./Science Source; 130: Steve Bloom
Images/Superstock, Inc.; 131: Steve Downeranth/
Pantheon/Superstock, Inc.; 132: NHPA/Superstock,
Inc.; 133: Doptis/Thinkstock; 134: Gallo Images/
Martin Harvey/Getty Images; 134 speedometer
icons: chilly_minnesota/iStockphoto; 135: Georgie
Holland/age fotostock; 136: Tom Brakefield/Getty
Images; 137: Jesse Kraft/Dreamstime; 138-139:
WLDavies/iStockphoto; 140: Paul Nicklen/Getty
Images; 141: Brandon Cole Marine Photography;
142: Joanne Weston/Dreamstime; 143: James D.
Watt/Seapics.com; 144: f11photo/Shutterstock; 145:
STR/AP Images; 146: Ksumano/Dreamstime; 147:
kikkerdirk/Thinkstock; 148: William D. Bachman/
Science Source; 149: Jim Zipp/Getty Images; 150:
nikpal/Thinkstock; 151: Tim Layman/Getty Images;
152: prasit_chansareekorn/iStockphoto; 153: Art
Wolfe/Science Source; 154: Chris Knightsan/
Pantheon/Superstock, Inc.; 155: Jonathan Irish/Getty
Images; 156-157: Bernard Breton/Dreamstime; 158:
teptong/iStockphoto; 159: Stephen Dalton/Minden
Pictures/Superstock, Inc.; 160: Roger Eritja/age
fotostock; 161: Piotr Naskrecki/Minden Pictures/
Getty Images; 162 top: ZJAN/Supplied by WENN.
com/Newscom; 162 bottom: Simon Maycock/Alamy
Stock Photo; 163 top dog: Wasitt Hemwarapornchai/

Shutterstock; 163 top cat: Andrey_Kuzmin/ Shutterstock; 163 center: Wilfredo Lee/AP Images; 163 bottom: Geoff Dann/Getty Images; 164: Betty Chu; 165: Spencer Platt/Getty Images; 166: Seth Wenig/AP Images; 167: cynoclub/iStockphoto; 168: Matt Writtle/Barcroft Media/Getty Images; 169 background: Hsc/Dreamstime; 169 dog: GlobalP/ Thinkstock; 170: alexytrener/Thinkstock; 171: Jana Mackova/Shutterstock; 172-173: David McNew/ Getty Images; 174 top: Ulises Ruiz Basurto/EPA-EFE/ Shutterstock; 174 bottom: Calvin L. Leake/ Dreamstime; 175 top: Albert Gonzalez Farran/AFP/ Getty Images; 175 center: Danny Lawson/PA Images/Getty Images; 175 bottom: Niall_Majury/ Getty Images; 176: p-orbital/Thinkstock; 177: petrenkoua/Thinkstock; 178: Suzanne Tucker/Getty Images; 179: Charles Bowman/age fotostock; 180: Bokgallery/Dreamstime; 181: Digoarpi/Dreamstime; 182-183: Stephen Alvarez/National Geographic Creative; 184: Tom Tweedy/De Beers; 185: Nguyen-Anh Le/discopalace.com/Getty Images; 186 climber icon: Robert Adrian Hillman/Shutterstock; 187: Pete Atkinson/Getty Images; 188: Valentin Armianu/Dreamstime; 189: NASA; 190: Imagineimages/Dreamstime; 191: stellaristock/ iStockphoto; 192 top: Gerben Van Es/AFP/Getty Images; 192 bottom: NurPhoto/Getty Images; 193 top: Kyodo News/Getty Images; 193 center: jamesjagger/StockimoNews/Alamy Stock Photo; 193 bottom: Sekkouri Kamel/Geoff Robinson Photography/Shutterstock; 194: Dean Conger/Getty Images; 195: Daniel Kreher/imageBROKER/age fotostock; 196-197: David McNew/Getty Images; 198: Tigeryan/iStockphoto; 199: eyecrave/ iStockphoto; 200: Michele Cornelius/Dreamstime; 201: Everett Collection/age fotostock; 202: Wang xizeng/AP Images; 203: CampPhoto/iStockphoto; 204: Nadine Spires/Dreamstime; 205: Dark Moon Pictures/Shutterstock; 206-207: Tamir Kalifa/AP Images; 208 top: Luciano Mortula/Dreamstime; 208 bottom: Ferrari/ZUMA Press/Newscom; 209 top: Emanuele Cremaschi/Getty Images; 209 center: Lisa Howeler/Alamy Stock Photo; 209 bottom: Andrew Barker/Alamy Stock Photo; 210: Dan Anderson/ ZUMA Press/Newscom; 211: Alaska Stock/age fotostock; 211 plane icons: Walking-onstreet/ Shutterstock; 212: Russ Kinne/age fotostock; 213: PODIS/Shutterstock; 213 diamonds: Gems Collection/Shutterstock; 214: Sam Gangwer/ZUMA Press/Newscom; 215: aznature/Thinkstock; 216: Randy Duchaine/Alamy Stock Photo; 217: Newman Mark/age fotostock; 218: Lequint/Dreamstime; 219: Anneka/Shutterstock; 220: Lucy Pemoni/AP Images; 221: Icon Sports Wire/Getty Images; 222: Nagel Photography/Shutterstock; 223: Buyenlarge/Getty Images; 224: Don Smetzer/Alamy Stock Photo; 225: Keith Kapple/Superstock, Inc.; 226: Stephen J. Cohen/Getty Images; 227: John CancalosiPan/ Pantheon/Superstock, Inc.; 228: johnwoodcock/ iStockphoto; 229: Dave Newman/Shutterstock; 230: Ramona Kaulitzki/Shutterstock; 231: Orange Vectors/Shutterstock; 232: Courtesy of Mall of America; 233: Courtesy of USA International Ballet Competition; 234: Paul Fearn/Alamy Stock Photo; 235: Edgloris E. Marys/age fotostock; 236: Robert_ Ford/iStockphoto; 237: Bob Thomason/Getty Images; 238: Courtesy of Nansen Ski Club; 239: Loop Images/Getty Images; 240: Courtesy of Las-cruces. org; 240 sky: detchana wangkheeree/Shutterstock; 241: RoadsideAmerica.com; 242: Alan Marler/AP Images; 243: StudioSmart/Shutterstock; 244: Library of Congress; 245: John Elk III/Getty Images; 246: Stas Moroz/Shutterstock; 247: Matt Rourke/AP Images; 248: Jerry Coli/Dreamstime; 249: Courtesy of Ed Currie; 250: Sergio Pitamitz/age fotostock; 251 center: Louella938/Shutterstock; 251 background: Christophe Boisson/Shutterstock; 252: Science Faction/Getty Images; 253: Johnny Adolphson/Dreamstime; 254: Tara Golden/ Dreamstime; 255: Frontpage/Shutterstock; 256: Kevin Schafer/Getty Images; 257: Jon Bilous/ Shutterstock; 258: Tom Lynn/Getty Images; 259: Richard Maschmeyer/age fotostock; 260-261: Heuler Andrey/AGIF/Shutterstock; 262 top: Lloyd Images/ Getty Images; 262 bottom: courtesy of Nike; 263 top: Bloomberg/Getty Images; 263 center: James Borchuck/ZUMA Press/Newscom; 263 bottom: Bizuayehu Tesfaye/AP Images; 264: ZJAN/Supplied by WENN.com/Newscom; 265: howridiculous.org; 266: Streeter Lecka/Getty Images; 267: Gian Ehrenzeller/Newscom; 268: Jason Enterline/ iStockphoto; 269: Chicago Tribune/Getty Images; 270: Focus on Sport/Getty Images; 271: Mark J. Terrill/AP Images; 272: Barry Gossage/Getty Images; 273: Frederick Breedon/Getty Images; 274: Tom Szczerbowski/Getty Images; 275: Greg Trott/AP Images; 276: Jerry Coli/Dreamstime; 277: Jerry Coli/ Dreamstime; 278: Kevork Djansezian/Getty Images; 279: Jed Jacobsohn/Getty Images; 280: Rich Graessle/AP Images; 281: Jamie Squire/Getty Images; 282: Transcendental Graphics/Getty Images; 283: Denis Poroy/AP Images; 284: Victor Decolongon/Getty Images; 285: Associated Press/AP Images; 285 tape: clsgraphics/iStockphoto; 286: Roberto Schmidt/AFP/Getty Images; 287: Guang Niu/Getty Images; 288: Chatchai Somwat/ Dreamstime; 289: Gregory Shamus/Getty Images; 290: Express/Getty Images; 291: Anja Niedringhaus/ AP Images; 292: Jared C. Tilton/Getty Image; 293: Associated Press/AP Images; 294: Ryan Remiorz/AP Images; 295: Jerry Coli/Dreamstime; 296: Rocky W. Widner/Getty Images; 297: Minas Panagiotakis/Getty Images; 298: Al Messerschmidt Archive/AP Images; 299: David Madison/Getty Images; 300: Marco Bertorello/AFP/Getty Images; 301: Popperfoto/Getty Images; 302: Mitchell Gunn/Dreamstime; 303: Zhukovsky/Dreamstime; 304: David Phillip/AP Images; 305: Aris Messinis/AFP/Getty Images; 306: Raphael Dias/Getty Images; 307: Buda Mendes/ Getty Images.

A MAGICAL
SUMMER OF READING

The 2018 Scholastic Summer Reading Challenge was one for the books! This summer, Scholastic encouraged kids to read every day, just for fun. Those reading minutes added up quickly, and this year's numbers proved it! From May 7 to September 7, 2018, kids in the U.S. read a whopping total of **135,865,170** minutes! That's the sixth year in a row kids logged more than 100 million minutes. **WOW!**

THESE ARE THE PRELIMINARY RESULTS FOR THE SUMMER READING CHALLENGE. TO FIND OUT MORE, PLEASE VISIT www.scholastic.com/summer/

CONGRATULATIONS TO EVERYONE WHO PARTICIPATED IN 2018!

STATES WITH THE MOST MINUTES READ
Did your state make the top 20?

Number of participating schools:
2,651

Number of schools logging 100,000 minutes or more:
264

STATES WITH THE MOST MINUTES READ:

1.	Texas	21,826,709
2.	Massachusetts	11,751,591
3.	California	8,860,042
4.	Florida	8,544,175
5.	New Jersey	8,536,733
6.	Pennsylvania	8,403,757
7.	New York	6,283,154
8.	Michigan	5,025,846
9.	North Carolina	4,852,640
10.	Louisiana	4,201,168
11.	Illinois	3,898,884
12.	Tennessee	3,670,498
13.	Kentucky	2,410,607
14.	Nebraska	2,332,576
15.	Washington	2,273,983
16.	New Mexico	2,214,577
17.	Maryland	2,175,210
18.	Colorado	2,043,648
19.	Idaho	2,016,329
20.	Maine	1,574,849

TOP SCHOOLS IN EACH STATE!

These schools all earned top honors by reading the most in their state.

Alabama	Mount Carmel Elementary School	Huntsville	109,645
Alaska	Sand Lake Elementary School	Anchorage	35,627
Arizona	American Leadership Academy - Ironwood	Queen Creek	744,356
Arkansas	The New School	Fayetteville	102,674
California	Warm Springs Elementary School	Fremont	2,793,070
Colorado	Prospect Ridge Academy	Broomfield	606,590
Connecticut	Scotland Elementary School	Scotland	183,836
Delaware	Wilson Elementary School	Newark	472,324
District of Columbia	Holy Trinity School	Washington	13,300
Florida	Liberty Park Elementary School	West Palm Beach	1,722,744
Georgia	Savannah Country Day School	Savannah	420,830
Hawaii	Laie Elementary School	Laie	386,847
Idaho	Peregrine Elementary School	Meridian	1,463,620
Illinois	Walnut Trails Elementary School	Shorewood	866,232
Indiana	Allisonville Elementary School	Indianapolis	452,732
Iowa	Resurrection Elementary School	Dubuque	331,121
Kansas	St. Thomas Aquinas School	Wichita	218,041
Kentucky	Lowe Elementary School	Louisville	927,084
Louisiana	Lisa Park Elementary School	Houma	3,265,541
Maine	Brewer Community School	Brewer	647,009
Maryland	Bradley Hills Elementary School	Bethesda	626,394
Massachusetts	James M. Quinn Elem School	North Dartmouth	1,369,474
Michigan	Daisy Brook Elementary School	Fremont	1,823,895
Minnesota	Maranatha Christian Academy	Brooklyn Park	516,812
Mississippi	Annunciation Catholic School	Columbus	782,335
Missouri	Spoede Elementary School	Saint Louis	312,191
Montana	Belgrade Middle School	Belgrade	56,892
Nebraska	Stuart Elementary School	Stuart	1,251,502
Nevada	Jan Jones Blackhurst Elementary School	Las Vegas	66,148
New Hampshire	Rochester Middle School	Rochester	289,125
New Jersey	Newell Elementary School	Allentown	1,544,625
New Mexico	University Hills Elementary School	Las Cruces	2,018,258
New York	Denton Avenue Elementary School	New Hyde Park	886,611
North Carolina	Ballantyne Elementary School	Charlotte	1,284,341
North Dakota	Erik Ramstad Middle School	Minot	436,791
Ohio	Mulberry Elementary School	Milford	271,687
Oklahoma	Hawthorne Elementary School	Oklahoma City	28,349
Oregon	Manzanita Elementary School	Grants Pass	296,864
Pennsylvania	South Elementary School	Trappe	1,603,769
Puerto Rico	Robinson School	San Juan	21,149
Rhode Island	Halliwell Memorial Elem School	North Smithfield	343,778
South Carolina	Oakridge Elementary School	Clover	342,851
South Dakota	Aberdeen Christian School	Aberdeen	153,861
Tennessee	Crosswind Elementary School	Collierville	1,169,623
Texas	H.D. Hilley Elementary School	El Paso	4,193,903
Utah	Freedom Academy	Provo	375,242
Vermont	Orwell Village School	Orwell	37,142
Virgin Islands	Joseph Gomez Elementary School	St. Thomas	30,747
Virginia	Ashburn Elementary School	Ashburn	157,932
Washington	Sunrise Elementary School	Spokane Valley	1,337,501
West Virginia	St. Francis Central Catholic School	Morgantown	851,165
Wisconsin	Riverdale Elementary-Middle School	Muscoda	468,049
Wyoming	Little Snake River Valley School	Baggs	63,734

TOP LIBRARIES AND COMMUNITY PARTNERS!

For the first time in 2017, Scholastic welcomed libraries and community partners to participate. Congratulations to the top libraries and top community partners!

LIBRARIES

	CITY & STATE
Pickford Community Library	Pickford, MI
Dustin Michael Sekula Memorial Library	Edinburg, TX
Okeechobee County Library	Okeechobee, FL
Gibson Library	Henderson, NV
Cupertino Public Library	Cupertino, CA
Seaford Public Library	Seaford, NY
Monmouth - Cumston Public Library	Monmouth, ME
Stayton Public Library	Stayton, OR
Gadsden County Public Library	Quincy, FL
Shawnee Public Library	Shawnee, OK

COMMUNITY PARTNERS

America Reads-Mississippi	Jackson, MS
Hollywood Community Housing	Los Angeles, CA

MILLION MINUTE READERS CLUB!

Outside of the "Best in State" schools, students at these schools reached this awesome milestone.

SCHOOLS	CITY & STATE	MINUTES
Parkland Middle School	El Paso, TX	4,062,409
Hirsch Elementary School	Fremont, CA	2,103,559
Horizon Heights Elementary School	Horizon City, TX	1,853,328
New River Elementary School	Wesley Chapel, FL	1,580,399
Pyne Arts Magnet School	Lowell, MA	1,273,773
Brooksville Elementary School	Brooksville, FL	1,116,534

THE SUMMER READING CHALLENGE GOES VIRAL!

Thousands of kids were excited about reading over the summer—and about choosing what they wanted to read. Check out these cool events, stats, and viral moments from the Challenge!

Illustrations by Jim Kay © 2015-2017 by Bloomsbury Publishing Plc.

A Magical Summer of Reading

The 2018 Scholastic Summer Reading Challenge celebrated the 20th anniversary of the release of *Harry Potter and the Sorcerer's Stone!*

The Scholastic Summer Reading Road Trip

Throughout the month of July, two colorfully designed **Summer Reading Road Trip** RVs toured across the U.S. to host "pop-up" reading festivals in collaboration with community organizations, bookstores, and public libraries. At each stop, kids and their families joined the summer learning fun by participating in hands-on activities, winning prizes, meeting their favorite authors and illustrators, and taking photos with special guests including Clifford the Big Red Dog®.

Reading Ambassadors

Oregon First Spouse Dan Little reads aloud to students.

To help provide more kids with access to books and to tackle the summer slide, 41 Governors' Spouses, 2 Governors and 1 Lieutenant Governor representing the U.S. states and territories signed on to serve as Reading Ambassadors for the **2018 Scholastic Summer Reading Challenge**. Each donated 500 Scholastic books to schools in their states and hosted read-aloud events to highlight the importance of summer learning.

Illustrations by Jim Kay © 2015-2017 by Bloomsbury Publishing Plc.

Minute Mania Month

Minute Mania Month ran from August 7 through the end of the Challenge on September 7, and kids broke the 100 million minute mark on August 13!

SCHOLASTIC.COM/SUMMER

Pickford Community Library Reads to the Top!

Pickford, MI has a population of 1,595, but they are amazing readers. Students at the local schools logged 338,057 reading minutes during the library's summer reading program. They used social media and lots of amazing prizes to reward top readers! Congratulations!

Sunrise Elementary School

Students at Sunrise Elementary, Spokane, WA, have been participating in the Summer Reading Challenge since 2012, and this year they finally reached the top in their state, reading 1,337,501 minutes!

Denton Avenue Elementary School

To read to the top in New York, the school created a kick off to summer reading event, which featured an author visit, goal setting, and distribution of Summer Reading Challenge usernames and passwords. Students also planned field trips to the local public library for all kindergarten students to obtain their library cards.

Show Your Four Sweepstakes!

Research shows children who read four or more books during the summer break fare better on reading comprehension tests when compared to their peers who read just one book (or none) over the summer. To get children (and adults) excited about summer reading, we asked them to show us four (or more) books they were most excited to read this summer for a chance to win a magical summer reading book box.